W9-AGB-477

THE GOOD, THE BAD, AND THE UGLY
MINNESOTA VIKINGS

HEART-POUNDING, JAW-DROPPING, AND GUT-WRENCHING MOMENTS FROM MINNESOTA VIKINGS HISTORY

Steve Silverman

TRIUMPH
BOOKS

To Judy, Samantha, and Gregory, my own All-Pro team.

To Gloria and Stanley, you've always been with me.

Library of Congress Cataloging-in-Publication Data

Silverman, Steve, 1956–
    The good, the bad, and the ugly Minnesota Vikings / Steve Silverman.
        p. cm.
    ISBN-13: 978-1-57243-988-7
    ISBN-10: 1-57243-988-2
    1. Minnesota Vikings (Football team)—History. I. Title.

GV956.M5S55 2007
796.332'6409776579—dc22

                                                                2007009850

This book is available in quantity at special discounts for your group or organization. For further information, contact:

Triumph Books
542 South Dearborn Street
Suite 750
Chicago, Illinois 60605
(312) 939-3330
Fax (312) 663-3557

Printed in U.S.A.
ISBN: 978-1-57243-988-7
Design by Patricia Frey
All photos courtesy of AP/Wide World Photos.

CONTENTS

FOREWORD

The Minnesota Vikings have been anything but an ordinary franchise since coming into existence in 1961.

Far from getting hammered in their first NFL game, the Vikings achieved a substantial upset of George Halas and the Chicago Bears when a young quarterback named Fran Tarkenton came off the bench and led the team to victory.

The Vikings were making headlines even before that game and have gone on to achieve a noteworthy record. In the beginning they were supposed to join Lamar Hunt in the American Football League, but in a plot worthy of a Hollywood script, a last-second deal with Halas and the NFL switched them to the more established NFL. Soon they were among the league's great powers, winning the NFL championship in 1969 and playing in Super Bowl IV. Sadly, instead of becoming their crowning moment, the game turned into a pummeling by the AFL's Kansas City Chiefs led by Head Coach Hank Stram.

Bud Grant, Alan Page, Carl Eller, Jim Marshall, and Joe Kapp are just a few of the names that allowed this franchise to rise from expansion team to pulverizing power in a matter of a few short years. Throughout the 1970s they played in the Super Bowl four times, only to fall short each time. While the cynics may say the Vikings didn't win the big game, the four losses came against the Chiefs, the Dolphins, the Steelers, and the Raiders—all teams that rank among the all-time greats.

While the team has not been back to the big game since Super Bowl XI, the excitement has not come close to stopping. Headliners like Cris Carter, Randall Cunningham, Keith Millard, and Joey Browner have kept the tradition alive.

I had the privilege of playing for the Vikings in the 1990s under Head Coach Denny Green, and while we may not have won every game, we were capable of putting the fear of God into every opponent we came up against.

The Vikings have been a lot of things in the NFL, but one thing they have never been is boring. They have had their share of ups, downs, sad times, and thrilling moments—and in this book, veteran writer and broadcaster Steve Silverman has captured those moments for all Vikings fans to relive and enjoy.

Not only did Steve do a great job of bringing to life the headline-making moments of the past, he also tells the stories with the passion that all Vikings fans feel for their team.

And the stories are worth telling. The heartbreak of the Super Bowl losses has never waned. It is reminiscent of another storied team in another sport—Major League Baseball's Boston Red Sox. Like the Vikings, the Red Sox had been tortured by coming close and enduring years of futility when it came to winning a championship. That torture finally ended in 2004 with a four-game sweep of the St. Louis Cardinals in the World Series.

Hopefully, the Vikings will have their own moment in the sun in the not-too-distant future.

—Sean Salisbury
May 2007

ACKNOWLEDGMENTS

My journey in covering professional football began with a love of sports from the early days of childhood.

The switch was flipped for me at the age of eight when I became aware of the thrill of competition and the wonders of pro sports. It started during the 1964 World Series when I saw Mickey Mantle hit a game-winning home run in the bottom of the ninth inning, and my interests soon grew to include football.

Jim Brown, Bart Starr, and Dick Butkus were my heroes, and the complexity and color of the sport were amazing. The charisma of a head coach like Vince Lombardi and the determination of Lamar Hunt in starting a new league only cemented my interest in the game.

My first experience covering the game came for a medium-sized newspaper in New Brunswick, New Jersey, called *The Home News*. I was a young sportswriter when the sports editor called a meeting in the fall of 1981. He laid out the expectations of the sports department and the newspaper's rules and regulations. As the meeting was about to end, he said he had one other piece of business. "We are covering the Giants," he lamented. "Does anyone want to cover the game this week?"

My hand couldn't go up fast enough. To think that such an opportunity was presented as if it was a burden was amazing.

Nobody else wanted the gig. I covered the Giants against the St. Louis Cardinals that fall Sunday in 1981 and many of the other

Giants games as well. Lawrence Taylor was a rookie, Bill Parcells was an assistant coach, and Phil Simms was struggling with inconsistency. The Giants made the playoffs that season for the first time in 18 years, and it was sheer excitement when they beat the Cowboys in the season finale on a field goal by Joe Danelo in overtime. The franchise was on its way toward a return to glory.

A few years later I became immersed in my career while working for Hub Arkush at *Pro Football Weekly*. Along with writers and editors like Rick Korch, Bob LeGere, Michael Lev, Ron Pollack, Neil Warner, Keith Schleiden, Dan Arkush, and the late Joel Buchsbaum, I worked on a great paper that remains so to this day.

College and Pro Football Newsweekly editors Peter Hayes and Vic DeNicola have continued to give me an opportunity to write about pro football. MSNBC.com's George Malone and Mike Miller have also given me a forum that I truly appreciate.

A career in radio also came to fruition with much thanks going to Dan McNeil and Ron Gleason for giving me an opportunity to work at WSCR-AM in Chicago. I had a chance to work with great pros like Doug Buffone, Jesse Rogers, Jonathan Hood, Fred Huebner, and Raymont Harris, and I loved the raucous atmosphere. Dan Zampillo has continued to let me speak out on WXYT-AM in Detroit.

Colleagues like Allen Barra and Allen St. John have given me opportunities to expand my horizons and improve my craft. Both are outstanding writers and good friends.

Triumph Books editor Tom Bast has given me a chance to write this book on a tremendous subject like the Minnesota Vikings. I appreciate the opportunity and the chance to work with Triumph's tremendous staff. Doing the research on this legendary team led me to reconnect with Joe Horrigan of the Pro Football Hall of Fame along with that institution's Pete Fierle and Saleem Choudhry.

Additionally, my research involved information gleaned from the following excellent sources: *Purple Hearts and Golden Memories: 35 Years With The Minnesota Vikings*, by Jim Klobuchar; *Tarkenton*, by Fran Tarkenton and Jim Klobuchar; *One More July: A Football Dialogue with Bill Curry*, by George Plimpton; *Total Football: The*

Official Encyclopedia of the National Football League, by Bob Carroll, Michael Gershman, David Neft, and John Thorn; *False Glory: The Steve Courson Story,* by Steve Courson and Lee R. Schreiber; *Interference: How Organized Crime Influences Professional Football,* by Dan E. Moldea; *The Making of the Super Bowl: The Inside Story of the World's Greatest Sporting Event,* by Don Weiss and Chuck Day; *The Pro Football Chronicle,* by Dan Daly and Bob O'Donnell; *The History of the Super Bowl,* by Austin Murphy; *Big Play: Barra on Football,* by Allen Barra; *Inside the Helmet: A Player's Eye View of the NFL,* by Peter King; *Inside Quarterbacking,* by Len Dawson; *America's Game: The Epic Story of How Pro Football Captured a Nation,* by Michael MacCambridge; *Papa Bear: The Life and Legacy of George Halas,* by Jeff Davis; *Hard Knox: The Life of an NFL Coach,* by Chuck Knox and Bill Plaschke; *Sports Illustrated*; *Pro Football Weekly*; the Minneapolis *StarTribune*; the *St. Paul Pioneer Press*; NFL.com; Vikingunderground.com; and Purplepride.org. I thank them all for their insightful and intelligent work.

Finally, I would like to thank my wife, Judy, who has always supported my career and my dreams. Her encouragement, criticisms, and spirit have always served as inspirations.

INTRODUCTION

The Minnesota Vikings have been playing football since 1961, and their history is rich with achievement and heartbreak. They have not won a Super Bowl, but they have had some of the greatest players the game has ever seen and one coach who ranks with the all-time greats.

Fran Tarkenton was one of the most innovative quarterbacks the game has ever seen. When he started his career with the Vikings after a stellar career at Georgia, he had to prove himself to rookie head coach Norm Van Brocklin. Tarkenton demonstrated early on that he could be a star in the league, but he never impressed his coach, who had enjoyed a Hall of Fame career as a quarterback himself.

Tarkenton nevertheless endured, was traded to New York, and then came back to the Vikings to put a brilliant capper on his career. The year Tarkenton was traded to the Giants, Bud Grant accepted owner Max Winter's offer to become head coach. Grant had originally been offered the job before Van Brocklin, but he turned it down because he was a successful coach in the Canadian Football League and wanted to honor his obligation to the Winnipeg Blue Bombers.

But once he became a part of the franchise, the Vikings went from expansion team to perennial contender. The base of the team was a marauding defense that was on a search-and-destroy mission on an every-week basis. Was there ever a front four like the Purple People Eaters? They didn't care about sack dances or celebrations. They did it with speed, power, technique, and intelligence. When Jim Marshall identified the unit's goal—"Let's Meet at the Quarterback"—that's just what they did.

The Vikings became one of the elite teams in the NFL, reaching the Super Bowl four times—and falling short each time. True Vikings fans have never lost hope that their team will get back to the Super Bowl and win it, but they have yet to return since losing to the Oakland Raiders in Super Bowl XI.

This team has known heartbreak—much like the Boston Red Sox had before they finally won the World Series in 2004—but they have also known brilliance and achievement.

They have a rich history, and it has been my pleasure to relive it by going through the archives at the Pro Football Hall of Fame and by talking to scouts, players, and coaches who played for and competed against them.

From their initial season, the Vikings have been anything but predictable. Check that. From *before* their initial season, they have been anything but predictable. The Minnesota franchise was one of the original members of the "Foolish Club" and was set to join the American Football League in 1960. However, they turned their backs on the new league when Chicago Bears owner George Halas and the NFL came calling.

That one move was one of the most telling events in pro football history. The AFL owners had plenty of motivation to succeed when nobody thought they would. But when Minnesota left Lamar Hunt and his band of renegades standing in the lurch, their determination to succeed and survive reached a new level.

The Vikings have been one of the most pivotal franchises in the history of the NFL, both on the field and off it. Some of it good, some of it bad, and some of it ugly.

But all of it fascinating.

IN THE BEGINNING

AFL OR NFL?

The Vikings entered the NFL as an expansion team in 1961, one year after the Dallas Cowboys began play.

But instead of joining the established NFL, Minnesota nearly became one of the founding teams in the American Football League. The move from one league to the other helped fuel the war between the AFL and NFL during the first half of the 1960s.

Before we get into the details, here's the back story.

During the second half of the 1950s, it was clear that professional football was a sport on the rise. It was still behind professional baseball, but the national pastime was growing stiff and stale. With each passing season, football was taking more of a hold on a growing group of fans that just couldn't get enough of it.

But there was a problem. There were 12 teams in the NFL and none of the owners were interested in expanding to cities like Minneapolis, Dallas, Denver, and Houston, which desperately wanted franchises. Chicago Bears owner George Halas and Washington Redskins owner George Preston Marshall were especially firm in not wanting to expand—and nothing got done in the NFL if Halas wasn't behind the idea.

Bert Bell might have been the commissioner of the NFL, but Halas was the true power in the league. Bell made sure he never got into any wars with the crusty Bears owner because he was

1

more of a pat-you-on-the-back, "attaboy" type of guy. Bell felt he owed Halas his loyalty because the "old man" had gotten Bell the job of commissioner. Additionally, confrontation was never his style—especially with a curmudgeon like Halas.

Despite Halas's and the other owners' reluctance to change the status quo, there were plenty of inquiries made about expansion or acquiring an existing franchise. The Chicago Cardinals were struggling badly with 84 defeats and monetary losses of more than $1 million in the 1950s. Cardinals owner Vi Bidwill and her husband Walter Wolfner were considering moving out of the south side of the city, where the team was getting pounded by Halas's Bears.

Bell was hoping Bidwill and Wolfner would either sell or move their franchise, but they resisted all suitors and decided to keep the team. That didn't stop Lamar Hunt, a young businessman who was the son of oil magnate H.L. Hunt. He had been transfixed by the 1958 championship game between the Giants and the Colts, and as he watched the Colts win the overtime game in Yankee Stadium, his interest in pro football became an obsession.

He went to the Cardinals owners and made them a lucrative offer, but they wouldn't sell. Hunt then went to Bell and asked for an expansion franchise and was told that it was not going to happen.

That did not stop Hunt. On the flight back home to Dallas, he decided he was not going to be sidetracked by men like Halas, Marshall, and Bell. If he could not buy an NFL team or get an expansion team, he would start his own league. He knew that Bud Adams in Houston hungered to get into professional football, as did Max Winter, a Minnesota businessman who owned the NBA's Minneapolis Lakers.

Hunt put together eight prospective founding members of the American Football League. The franchises were to be located in Dallas, Houston, Buffalo, New York City, Los Angeles, Boston, Denver, and Minneapolis. The Minnesota franchise was considered especially valuable because it would give the AFL control of the upper Midwest area. This was something that would get under

Representatives of the fledgling American Football League pose in New York City on October 28, 1959, less than a month before Max Winter and his Minneapolis partners abandoned ship and accepted a late offer to join the National Football League. Posing in the front row are (from left) Robert L. Howsam, Denver; Winter; league founder Lamar Hunt, Dallas; and Bud Adams, Jr., Houston. In the back row are (from left) Barron Hilton, Los Angeles; Ralph C. Wilson Jr., Buffalo; and Harry Wismer, New York.

the skin of Halas because he did not want to see that area go to the new league. The threat of a new league coming to the Bears' turf would eventually start to fester and push Halas into action.

Bell had no opposition to the new league. He understood that owners might not be happy about competition, but he also knew the NFL had never grown more or had earned more publicity than when it battled with All-American Football Conference in the late 1940s. He thought a new league would only improve and grow a product that the American sports fans were eating up. Bell was

BUILDING A FOUNDATION

The Vikings showed signs right from their winning debut against the Chicago Bears that they would not be any ordinary expansion team. Norm Van Brocklin might not have been well-loved by his players, but he demanded results.

Fran Tarkenton gave his team the kind of quarterback play that no expansion team has had before or since. Bill Brown was a pulverizing full-back who dished out punishment rather than absorbing it. He might have looked like a Neanderthal, but he was actually quite graceful and could catch passes with the best running backs. Paul Flatley gave Tarkenton an outside receiving threat and Tommy Mason was a big-time playmaker as well.

The Vikings had losing records in their first three seasons, but things turned around dramatically in 1964. They started the season with a 34–24 win over the Baltimore Colts, a team that would eventually win the NFL's Western Conference with a 12–2 record. That victory ignited the team to believe in itself. Tarkenton would outduel Johnny Unitas with help from Mason, who opened the scoring with a spectacular 51-yard run in the first quarter.

The Vikings lost their next two games to the Bears and Rams, but then came a huge shocker. They beat the Packers 24–23 on the road in an effort that caught the attention of the rest of the league—and Green Bay coach Vince Lombardi. Brown had two short touchdown runs and Tarkenton threw a scoring pass to backup wideout Tom Hall.

The game came down to a final drive that Tarkenton handled with aplomb and kicker Fred Cox won the game with a 27-yard field goal late in the fourth quarter.

"That was a game that got his attention," said Packers All-Pro guard Jerry Kramer about his legendary coach. "He was angry with mistakes after we won a game, but to lose at home to this 'expansion' team was more than he could take. He was not happy with anything about the way we played and it made life very uncomfortable for the next week."

If the Vikings had gained confidence from their win over the Colts, the victory at Green Bay meant even more because it was on the road. The

Vikings no longer were an expansion team. They went on to finish with an 8–5–1 record, tying Green Bay for second in the Western Conference.

Tarkenton finished as the second-leading quarterback in the league, throwing for 2,506 yards with 22 touchdowns passes and 11 interceptions. He had plenty of help from Brown, who finished as the league's fourth-leading rusher with 866 yards and 7 touchdowns. He also caught 48 passes for 703 yards and a remarkable 9 touchdowns.

Even more notably, the first signs of the great Vikings defense would begin to show up. Jim Marshall led the team with 11.5 sacks, while rookie defensive end Carl Eller chipped in with 7.5 more.

The Vikings slipped to 7–7 in 1965 and followed that with two losing seasons in 1966 and '67. That would be the end of the losing. Minnesota finished 8–6 in 1968 and would not have a losing season again until 1979. The Vikings had arrived and the seeds of their winning ways had been planted in 1964, their first winning season.

actually quite helpful in advising Hunt on how to set up the new league and he sent Adams a business plan to use as a blueprint.

But when Bell died in 1959 of a heart attack while attending a Philadelphia Eagles game, Hunt knew that the rules had changed. Would men like Halas and Marshall welcome the competition? Of course not.

The NFL didn't waste any time before getting ready for the battle. A few weeks after Bell's death, the NFL changed its course and announced plans to expand to Dallas and Houston, in direct competition with Hunt and Adams. The NFL immediately tried to make peace by offering the expansion franchises to Hunt and Adams, but they weren't having it. Hunt, who had dreamed up and planned the league, was not about to leave his partners in the lurch even if the NFL was offering them what they had always wanted.

The AFL had its first meeting in a Chicago hotel room in August 1959, and then met again in November in Minneapolis to conduct its first draft. The night before that draft, the owners gathered together at the Cedric Adams Hotel for a scheduled meeting. Winter was representing the Minnesota franchise and he was clearly uneasy. None of the other owners knew why, but they would learn shortly.

Harry Wismer, the owner of the New York franchise, burst through the doors of the banquet room with a newspaper in hand. He was clearly angry and upset, nearly ready to explode.

One of the other owners asked Wismer if he was ready for dinner.

Wismer hesitated for a second. He looked around the room dramatically and answered the question. "Yes, and this is the last supper," Wismer yelled. "And there's Judas."

Wismer lifted his arm and pointed a finger at Winter. He slammed his newspaper down on the table for all of the owners to see. A huge headline blared "Minneapolis to Get NFL Franchise."

The NFL had problems securing a stadium in Houston, so it decided to go after Minneapolis. In surreptitious meetings with Halas, the Minnesota ownership group, which included Winter, Ole Haugsrud, Bill Boyer, Bernie Ridder, and H.P. Skoglund, took advantage of the NFL's expansion invitation and turned its back on its AFL partners.

TRIVIA

In what years did Les Steckel coach and what was his record?

Find the answers on pages 193–194.

Haugsrud's story is an interesting one. He was a Minneapolis insurance executive who owned the Duluth Eskimos in the 1920s. The NFL had given him an option contract to buy 10 percent of the franchise if the league ever decided to go back to Minnesota. He took advantage of that opportunity with Winter's group.

The negotiations to get the Minnesota group to drop its application to the AFL were like a scene out of *The Twilight Zone*. Halas initiated the meetings and was cordial, charming, and generally caring. Normally, Halas was irascible and demanding, but he was as shrewd an owner as there ever was in the NFL. The league would not see his type again until it merged with the AFL and Oakland Raiders owner Al Davis made his presence felt.

Halas convinced the Minnesota group to change affiliations by promising a roster full of players that would come to them in the expansion draft. That idea appealed to Winter and his co-owners, who would have had to start from scratch if they had stayed with the AFL.

While not all of the owners were as visibly upset as Wismer, the group felt blindsided and betrayed by Winter's group. The AFL moved on, later adding Oakland to take Minnesota's place.

But after enduring the initial shock of their betrayed partners, the Minnesota franchise moved ahead. On January 27, 1960, they formally withdrew their application to join the AFL. The next day, Minneapolis was granted an NFL expansion franchise at the league's winter meeting in Miami.

They joined the Dallas Cowboys as the NFL's first true expansion teams. The league had absorbed three franchises from the defunct All-American Football Conference in 1950, but the Cowboys and Vikings would start from scratch. The Cowboys started play in 1960, but the Vikings had an extra year to prepare before starting in 1961.

A DEBUT TO SHOUT ABOUT

Talk about coming in with a bang. The Vikings started their initial season with a home game against George Halas and the Chicago Bears. The Vikings had lost all of their preseason games and looked dreadful in the process. The Bears were in the upper echelon with more tradition than any team in the league.

Halas expected his team to go up to Metropolitan Stadium in Bloomington and administer a beating to the expansion team. He had every reason to think that would happen. The NFL had admitted the Dallas Cowboys the year before and they went winless in their initial season.

The Bears might have taken the Vikings a bit lightly at first, but it was clear early on that the expansion team was primed for a grand opening. While the crowd of 32,236 disappointed general manager Bert Rose, the play of his team did not. The Vikings rolled to a 37–13 victory that shocked Halas and set a standard for expansion teams that has never been approached.

The Vikings surprised head coach Norm Van Brocklin and Rose by playing such a sharp game. They started slowly with a 12-yard field goal by place-kicker Mike Mercer in the first quarter, but the team was not responding to quarterback George Shaw. Van Brocklin looked at rookie quarterback Fran Tarkenton, turned away, and then signaled the future Hall of Famer into the game.

Tarkenton responded with a 14-yard touchdown pass to Bob Schnelker in the second quarter. That served notice that the Bears were in for a real test. The Bears answered with a 3-yard touch-down run by Rick Casares, but place-kicker Roger LeClerc missed the extra point. The Vikings took a 10–6 lead into the locker room at halftime.

Halas blew a gasket in the visitors' locker room, screaming and yelling at his players in an effort to avoid the embarrassment of losing to a team playing its first game. But the hissy fit did not do the Bears any good at all. The Vikings scored two touchdowns in the third quarter. One of them came on a spectacular 29-yard catch by end Jerry Reichow and the other was Tarkenton's third touchdown pass of the day, a 2-yarder to Hugh McElhenny.

The Vikings stretched their lead to 31–10 in the fourth quarter when Tarkenton ran two yards for a score and Tarkenton added a fourth touchdown pass later in the quarter when he hit wide receiver Dave Middleton with another two-yard scoring pass.

The Bears finally scored late in the fourth quarter, but it could not alter the fact that they had been taken apart in the season opener by an expansion team.

Tarkenton and Van Brocklin were ecstatic in the Vikings locker room; the mood was more like that of a team that had just won the championship rather than one that had just won the first game of the season. Van Brocklin had hopes that his offense would continue to be productive and the defense just might be able to hold its own.

The Bears were humiliated with the defeat. Halas kept the doors of the locker room closed for nearly half an hour after the game in order to upbraid his team and cool off before reporters came in. When he finally relented and the press entered the Bears' locker room, Halas looked like a man in shock.

Rookie quarterback Fran Tarkenton poses during practice on September 19, 1961, two days after coming off the bench to throw four touchdown passes in a shocking upset of the Chicago Bears—the first game ever played by the Vikings.

"I've been with the Bears 42 years and I've never seen anything like it," Halas said. "I give the Vikings credit for capitalizing on our mistakes, but I have never seen so many things go wrong for our football team as they did in this game."

As embarrassed as Halas was, it didn't stop him from being a sportsman. He ran across the field and greeted Van Brocklin with a warm handshake and words of encouragement. "This is a big, big day for you and you'll never forget it."

Bears players were sheepish as they spoke with reporters, but they also credited the Vikings with an excellent effort. "I thought something like this could happen," said Casares, sensing the overconfidence that the Bears took with them when they left Chicago. "The Vikings threw a bold challenge right at us in the first quarter and we never answered it."

After Halas had made his comments to the press, he turned his attention back to his team. He continued to seethe as they prepared to leave Metropolitan Stadium and board a flight back to Chicago. He was so angry and so vindictive that he refused to allow his players to have any drinks on the plane. We're not talking about alcoholic beverages—he wouldn't even allow them to have a soft drink or water.

Tarkenton was clearly the star of the game. He connected on 17-of-23 passes for 250 yards in addition to his four touchdowns and he did not throw an interception. The 21-year-old Tarkenton wore a huge smile for days after the game and there was talk that the Vikings might be able to play competitive football that first season.

That idea turned out to be unrealistic. The Vikings lost their next seven games before they beat the Baltimore Colts 28–20 at the Met in November. They would add a December win over the Los Angeles Rams and finish with a 3–11 record.

While the Vikings were not winners, they did play an exciting brand of offense with Tarkenton starting the rest of the year at quarterback. His scrambling style not only produced excitement and several big plays, it also kept him upright as he avoided big hits that most likely would have knocked other quarterbacks out of action.

"I remember there was a lot of running that season and most of the time I was running for my life," Tarkenton said. "But in that first game, everything went right. It was just one of those things where it turned out to be our day and I will never forget it."

STADIUM STORIES: OUTDOOR CHARM, INDOOR HARM

Have you ever noticed how time romanticizes everything? This is particularly true in sports.

In Boston, they talk about the good old days when the Celtics and Bruins played in the "good old" Boston Garden—even though there were rats running around the arena.

In New York, the old timers talk about the days of Ebbets Field in Brooklyn. "Those were the good, old days, when there were intimate stadiums and you knew the name of the usher," even if the seats were 18 inches wide and the bathrooms reeked of urine on hot summer days.

TRIVIA

Two Vikings tight ends played in more than 100 games. Who are they?
Find the answers on pages 193–194.

Tiger Stadium was the home of both the Lions and the Tigers. Ernie Harwell broadcast baseball games there and Alex Karras sacked quarterbacks there. Yet how could the fans in the stands enjoy what they were seeing when they were sitting behind huge metal posts that kept the stadium standing?

Sports fans tend to look down on newer stadiums after a while because they often lack the intimacy of the older stadiums. However, they have all the modern conveniences that make the experience a lot more enjoyable to nearly everyone.

In the case of the Vikings, however, the change in stadiums from open-air Metropolitan Stadium to the Metrodome had a huge impact. When the team played at the old Met, the open-air stadium was a huge advantage. When the Vikings hosted games in November and December, they had the advantage of playing in the elements. Visiting teams clearly did not enjoy playing when the weather turned wintry, but the Vikings and their fans loved it.

They knew how to bear it. Playing outside gave the Vikings a tougher, more macho image. They were an outdoor, cold-weather team and nothing bothered them. Bud Grant built his team to be sturdier in the conditions. He wanted his team to relish playing outdoors in wintry conditions and would not allow heaters on the sidelines unless conditions were considered dangerous.

Grant said the image of a frozen Metropolitan Stadium may have been true for a few playoff games and at other times as well, but the weather was good for the majority of the games.

"You get the cold games with the winter conditions, but what about the games in September and October?" Grant asked. "It's

Calvin Griffith (top), president of the Minnesota Twins, in the press box at old Metropolitan Stadium on September 26, 1965, the day the Twins clinched the American League pennant. The Vikings and Major League Baseball's Minnesota Twins shared that stadium until moving into the Hubert H. Humphrey Metrodome (bottom) in 1982.

beautiful at that time of year here. November isn't bad either. The cold weather is somewhat overblown."

But there was no question about what visiting teams were going to get when they visited the Met. They would come face-to-face with a tough, physical, punishing defense and an offense that came at you any number of different ways. In short, the team was aggressive and sharp.

That was never more apparent than it was in the 1969 NFL championship game between the Vikings and the Browns at the Met. Cleveland was a hard team that had embarrassed the Cowboys 38–14 on the road and came into the Met with a full head of steam. Head coach Blanton Collier had a varied attack with Hall of Famer Leroy Kelly running the ball and a solid quarterback in Bill Nelsen throwing the ball to receivers Paul Warfield and Gary Collins.

The defense combined intelligence and aggressiveness. The Browns could not bring the same kind of athleticism and killer instinct that the Vikings had, but Collier thought he had a team that could win the game in the fourth quarter if it could stay close.

That may have been a nice idea, but the physical Vikings just pounded the Browns from the start and walked away with a 27–7 victory.

In the locker room of the cold and drafty Met, Carl Eller and Joe Kapp celebrated the victory with hugs and cigars. "You are my brother," Eller said to Kapp. "You and me, we are the same."

The two were extremely close friends even though Eller was an African American from South Carolina and Kapp was a Mexican American from California.

Jim Klobuchar, a columnist with the *Minneapolis Star-Tribune* for 30 years, observed the moment first hand and easily recalled it with eloquence and poignancy.

"Of all the memories I carried from the years when I wrote football, that scene is the engraving of what was right about the pro game if all of the sideshows and money glut of it were removed. This was a portrait of the athletic ideal in pro football. They *do* sacrifice," Klobuchar said. "Not all of them. The self-indulgence available to big-time athletes today overwhelms some

TRIVIA

Which Vikings kicker made the most field goals in a season?

Find the answers on pages 193–194.

of them. But the one permanent reality for Eller and Kapp on that day wasn't the television or the frenzy or even the money but the trust they placed in each other.

"A hard-knuckled, sweaty love *can* grow up among some of them, and it is never more vivid than on a frozen field when the reliance one man places in the man squatting and grunting beside him on the line of scrimmage is utter and complete.

"That might now be expressed in the past tense. The money today is enormous. So is the visibility."

The Vikings played their home games there from their 1961 debut season until it closed in 1981. They moved to the Metrodome in 1982 and it coincided with a change in the team's fortunes. The dominant team of the late 1960s and '70s had faded into memory and the Vikings of the 1980s were fighting for an identity. Their new surroundings certainly had a lot to do with the forging of that image.

The tough, marauding defense of the past had given way to a smaller and quicker one. An offensive line that was built to handle all elements and all conditions somehow lost its aura.

As romantic as the Old Met was in the hearts and minds of Vikings and Twins fans, the Metrodome has been labeled as cold and antiseptic. It provided an excellent home-field advantage for the Twins in World Series wins over the Cardinals and Braves in 1987 and 1991, respectively. The Twins won those World Series by sweeping their home games—and losing all six of the games they played on the road.

The Vikings were never able to establish that kind of advantage in the Metrodome. Even their dominant 1998 team, which had reeled off eight straight home wins by an average of 23.6 points per game, lost the NFC championship game at home in overtime to the Atlanta Falcons. Home-field mystique for the Vikings at the Metrodome? It was wiped out in that game if it ever existed at all.

It has proven to be an uncomfortable place to play because of all the noise that Vikings fans make, but the team has had a hard time sealing the deal. Chicago quarterback Rex Grossman said that he has never heard louder fans than he has at the Metrodome.

"You literally cannot hear anything in that place, not even the sound of your own voice," Grossman said. "It is the loudest place I have ever been in and the loudest place I have ever played in. Nothing is even close."

That noise confused Grossman in the Bears' Week 3 game at the Metrodome in 2006. Grossman's thought process became obscured early in the fourth quarter with the Bears playing in the shadow of their own goalposts. With the crowd roaring behind him, Grossman felt pressure from the Vikings front four. He threw a terrible pass in the right flat that was picked off by Antoine Winfield and returned seven yards for the go-ahead touchdown by the Vikings.

In the old days at the Met, a go-ahead touchdown by the defense in the fourth quarter would have ensured victory. But inside the Dome, nothing was guaranteed.

The Chicago defense got the ball back for Grossman in the late stages of the fourth quarter and he beat his tormentors with a 24-yard touchdown pass to Rashied Davis and only 1:53 remaining in the game.

"I never experienced such a wide swing of emotions in one quarter of football," Grossman said. "I made one of the worst throws ever at the start of the quarter and then got redemption with a good throw at the end. To do it against that team with that kind of noise was just unbelievable."

The fans brought da noise, but the Vikings could not bring da funk. That has been the story more often than not during the team's tenure in the Metrodome.

The Vikings are fighting and working to get a new outdoor stadium that would ensure that they stay in Minnesota for years to come. The plan is on the drawing board and needs to be approved by the Minnesota state legislature, so the team remains in the Metrodome and will stay there at least until their lease runs out after the 2011 season.

IN THE CLUTCH

TARKENTON: A QUARTERBACK ON THE RUN

Few players ever get a chance to go home again after getting traded. Fran Tarkenton did and he made the most of both of his runs with the Minnesota Vikings.

Tarkenton was drafted out of Georgia by the Vikings with their third-round pick in their initial draft in 1961. Even for that era, Tarkenton was considered small for the position. At 6'0" and 185 pounds (numbers that were likely overstated), he had a difficult time seeing over bigger defensive linemen when protection started to break down. In these situations, he did the only logical thing.

He took matters into his own hands and left the pocket when it was necessary. Sometimes Tarkenton would scramble left and throw, sometimes he would scramble right and throw, and sometimes he would take off and run. The style was effective and thrilling to the fans, but it annoyed Vikings head coach Norm Van Brocklin, who had been a Hall of Fame quarterback with the Rams and Eagles. Van Brocklin thought a quarterback needed to stay in the pocket to be effective and never truly appreciated Tarkenton's gifts. Van Brocklin was not one to act with political correctness or worry about anyone's feelings. Try telling him there was more than one way to do the job and you would be met with a stream of obscenities.

The Vikings traded Tarkenton to the New York Giants a month after Van Brocklin resigned in February 1967. Knowing they needed to add young talent, the team sent Tarkenton east for first- and second-round draft choices in 1967, a first-round choice in 1968, and a second-round choice in 1969. The Vikings made great use of those picks by taking running back Clint Jones and wide receiver Bob Grim in 1967, offensive tackle Ron Yary in

TRIVIA

Who was the first Vikings player to lead the team in both kickoff and punt returns?

Find the answers on pages 193–194.

1968, and offensive guard Ed White in 1969. Yary would go on to become one of the great blockers in the history of the NFL, and White was also a stalwart on the offensive line. He was widely recognized as one of the strongest men in the league. Jones was a solid all-around back who ran for 2,008 yards and 19 touchdowns. Grim was a solid role player with good hands.

Tarkenton's gifts were plentiful and he put them on display immediately. His first game was the team's debut against the powerful Bears in 1961. Instead of playing tentatively and getting pounded by their legendary rivals, Tarkenton relieved ineffective starting quarterback George Shaw early in the game and threw four touchdown passes and ran for a another to lead the Vikings to a 37–13 win. No expansion team has ever had such an impressive performance in its first game—before or since.

Tarkenton was a great leader who helped make the Vikings an exciting team in their early years, even if they did suffer the normal growing pains of an expansion team. His ability to escape pressure and buy time gave his receivers a chance to break containment and get open. Tarkenton made huge plays that would sometimes take 10–15 seconds to develop. NFL Films has reels and reels of Tarkenton highlights at its disposal.

Tarkenton learned his style of play as a youngster. His family moved to Athens, Georgia, when he was 11 years old in 1952 from Washington, D.C. He had started playing the game as a kid in the nation's capital and he did not find lush, green fields to play on.

"We played touch football every day," Tarkenton said, "and you had to be elusive because the alleys were narrow and you didn't have much room to dodge."

Fran Tarkenton, seen here unleashing a pass in the first half of an NFC playoff game against Dallas on December 28, 1975, was the original scrambler, eluding defenders in and out of the pocket to find time to get the ball downfield.

Tarkenton continued to climb the ladder after the move. He became a star quarterback at Athens High and led the team to a state championship in 1955.

Tarkenton had great stats as a college player at Georgia, but he will always be remembered for drawing a play in the dirt that won the Bulldogs an SEC title in 1959. Trailing Auburn 13–7, the conference championship hinged on the Bulldogs' ability to go downfield and score a touchdown. The Bulldogs had a 4th-and-goal play from the Auburn 13-yard line with 30 seconds left.

During a timeout, Tarkenton knelt beneath his offensive unit in the dirt and diagramed the play to show how Georgia was going to win the game.

Bobby Towns was in that now-famous huddle. "Coach [Wally] Butts had given us a play," Towns said. "But Francis said, 'Let's do this instead. I think it will work.'"

Tarkenton had done that before. A year earlier, as a sophomore, Tarkenton put himself into his first varsity game without consulting head coach Wally Butts.

"I had been pestering Coach Butts to let me go in because that was my personality," said Tarkenton, who ran on the field against Texas. "They wanted to redshirt me and I didn't want to because I thought I could help the team. So I just bolted onto the field. I put myself in."

Tarkenton drove his team 95 yards in an amazing 21 plays that culminated with a 3-yard touchdown pass to end Jimmy Vickers on third-and-goal.

That wasn't all. When Butts sent in the kicking unit, Tarkenton waved them off and went for two, hitting Aaron Box with a pass that put Georgia up 8–7.

That kind of past history gave his teammates confidence, so when he ignored the coach's play call against Auburn and drew up his play, the Dogs knew they were in good hands.

"I knew we needed something different," he said. "So what I designed in the huddle was a play where I was going to roll out to the right. I told the left end, Bill Herron, who was in tight—to really go ahead and make a block. I told him, 'Count to a thousand-four and then run to the left corner of the end zone."

Tarkenton sold the defense by rolling to the right while pretending to look for Towns. After counting a thousand-five, Tarkenton wheeled and let one sail to the left corner where a wide-open Herron made the catch for the touchdown.

The win gave Georgia the Southeastern Conference title and sent them to the Orange Bowl. It also opened the eyes of pro scouts and general managers, who started to believe Tarkenton could become an impact player in the NFL.

Tarkenton was nearly indestructible despite his small frame. He played nearly every game from 1961 through 1976 despite a slew of painful injuries that began to take their toll. However, the only serious injury he suffered in his career was a broken ankle in the 1977 season when he was hit by Cincinnati's Gary Burley. Tarkenton was carried off the field on a stretcher in that game and many believed that after 17 years in the league that he would call it a career.

But Tarkenton loved the game too much and still had a goal— the world championship that had eluded him and the franchise.

TARKENTON'S TOUGHEST DAY

As tough as Super Bowl losses were, the saddest day of Tarkenton's career had to come December 28, 1975. After a brilliant 12–2 season in which Tarkenton completed 273-of-425 passes for 2,994 yards with 25 touchdowns and 13 interceptions and won the league's offensive MVP award, the Vikings were viewed as the odds-on favorites to run through the NFC playoffs and get back to the Super Bowl where they would likely face the Steelers or the Raiders.

But an upstart team from Dallas had different ideas. Despite being overmatched at most positions, the Cowboys came into the postseason with no pressure as the NFC wild-card team. They had struggled in the first half of the season but the combination of Roger Staubach and Drew Pearson had helped them turn things around and lead a charge into the playoffs with a 10–4 record.

Grant knew that Tom Landry's Cowboys could never be taken lightly and that despite the frigid conditions at the Met, Dallas would not go away. They battled the Vikings on nearly even terms throughout the game. While the offense struggled to move the ball, the Cowboys defense did a good job of keeping Tarkenton & Co. from running them out of the stadium.

In the fourth quarter, the Vikings appeared to register the telling blow when Brent McClanahan scored on a 1-yard run in the fourth quarter. But Staubach would not quit. After converting a fourth-down play late in the final quarter, the Cowboys had a first down at midfield. With 32 seconds remaining, Staubach wound up and floated a deep pass down the right sideline. Cornerback Nate Wright had coverage on Drew Pearson, but the Vikings defensive back fell as the ball floated down. Pearson was able to make the catch and step into the end zone for the painful Dallas victory.

As bad as the defeat was, Tarkenton was dealt an even worse blow when he got the news that his father, Reverend Dallas Tarkenton, had died of a heart attack while watching the game. The loss of his father put the defeat in perspective for the Vikings quarterback, but it was still a disappointment.

He knew that age and injuries had taken a toll on him, and he thought about retiring for quite some time in the off-season. However, he swallowed hard and decided to return.

"I've had a lot of time to think about this since last season," he said in June 1978. "I don't want to be a shadow of my former self. I have been working out and I really want that Super Bowl ring. I may not be good enough to do that, but I play with 44 guys who are and we are going to give it one hell of a try."

Try they did, but the Vikings were a long way from the dominant team they had been in the late 1960s and most of the 1970s. They were somewhat competitive and barely qualified for the playoffs with an 8–7–1 record, but Tarkenton's career came to an unceremonious end when Minnesota dropped a 34–10 decision to the Rams in Los Angeles.

But between his brilliant opening act and quiet finale was a brilliant 18-year career that included 13 seasons with the Vikings and five with the Giants. When he retired, he left holding several notable records, including most games played by a quarterback (246), passing yards (47,003), touchdown passes (342), completions (3,686), attempts (6,467), and rushing yards (3,674). While Miami's Dan Marino went on to break most of these marks, all of Tarkenton's records lasted at least a decade.

Tarkenton's style that was criticized by Van Brocklin was appreciated by Bud Grant. When he came back to the Vikings for the final third of his career in 1972, he was a respected veteran who had suffered with some very bad Giants teams in New York. His Giants teams compiled a 33–37 record during Tarkenton's five seasons in New York and their failure to win even one spot in the postseason frustrated Tarkenton. However, if not for his presence on the team, the Giants would have been far worse. The Giants had few other stars besides Tarkenton, and he earned every one of those 33 wins in New York.

By 1972, the Vikings were a full-fledged NFL power. Quarterback Gary Cuozzo had led them to 12–2 and 11–3 records in 1970 and 1971, but the Vikings had been bounced out of the playoffs in the first round by the 49ers and Cowboys, respectively. Cuozzo was an effective quarterback, but when it came to rallying his teams and making a statement in the postseason, he simply lacked that ability. The Vikings went back to their roots and traded Norm Snead, Bob Grim, Vince Clements, a first-round draft pick, and a future third-round draft pick to re-acquire Tarkenton.

It was a great move for Tarkenton, who was going from one of the saddest teams in the league to one of the most powerful. While the Vikings' 1972 season was nothing special at 7–7, they would go to the playoffs the following six years with Tarkenton. Included in that streak were three appearances in the Super Bowl.

The Vikings did not win any of them and Tarkenton did not distinguish himself with his play in those games either. But all three of the opponents the Vikings lost to—the Steelers, Dolphins, and Raiders—were legendary teams who earned a spot in NFL folklore for their accomplishments. It would have taken superhuman efforts to beat the Dolphins or Raiders and moving the ball against Pittsburgh's Steel Curtain was nearly impossible.

TRIVIA

Who was the first 1,000-yard rusher for the Vikings, and in what year?

Find the answers on pages 193–194.

Tarkenton's legacy is not one of a quarterback who started and lost three Super Bowls. It is one of innovation and creativity. His style launched a new philosophy in the NFL that is still the norm and likely to remain so for a long time. Most quarterbacks may not be able to run like Tarkenton, but they all have to buy time with their feet in order to give their receivers time to make a play. Sitting in the pocket and hoping they get open quickly will get a quarterback crushed in a hurry.

Quarterbacks like Steve Young, Randall Cunningham, Daunte Culpepper, Doug Flutie, Michael Vick, and dozens of others were all influenced by Tarkenton's mobility and exciting style. Tarkenton was a smart, accurate, and personable leader whose talent belied the package that housed it. He was inducted into the Hall of Fame in 1986 and clearly deserved his spot in the shrine.

After leaving pro football, Tarkenton became a household name as an analyst on *Monday Night Football* and one of the co-hosts of the hit television series *That's Incredible!* After he left television, Tarkenton transferred his attention to the business world. He built his computer software company into a $129 million success story, even though he had issues when stocks plummeted and the company's problems prompted lawsuits.

Although he was knocked down, he got back up on his feet and remained in business. However, he will be remembered as a quarterback who could think on his feet and make big things happen for the Vikings. He was clearly an original who defied convention and succeeded in notable fashion.

THE NFL'S CAL RIPKEN

There are players all over the record books and history books that have not gotten their due. Just because a player might have been dominant at his position, had longevity, and left a giant footprint in his profession, it doesn't mean that he has a bust in Canton, Ohio, at the Pro Football Hall of Fame.

In many cities throughout the NFL, there are favorite sons who go unrewarded. The hue and cry in the nation's capital is louder for Art Monk's absence from the Hall than it is for the federal deficit. Raiders fans cannot believe that Ray Guy's legacy as a punter has not landed him in the Hall of Fame. Former Bears Richard Dent and Jimbo Covert were dominant players on a week-in, week-out basis but they are not in Canton.

All of these players have a great argument for getting into the Hall of Fame. But none of them have anything on Jim Marshall. Throughout his brilliant 20-year career, Marshall played consistently excellent football for perhaps the best defensive line of all time. If the Vikings needed a key stop on third-and-short, Marshall made the tackle. If they needed a late-game sack to squash a late rally, Marshall came around the corner. In moments of stress, Bud Grant and Norm Van Brocklin could count on Marshall to come through with the big play at the big moment.

The most amazing thing about Marshall's career might have been his ability to keep playing. Marshall played in 282 consecutive games—and never missed one throughout his time in the

NFL. The only player with more consecutive games played is punter Jeff Feagles, who had played in 304 straight games through the conclusion of the 2006 season.

But Feagles would be the first to tell you that his accomplishment pales when compared to Marshall's, for obvious reasons. You want to compare Marshall's longevity to another athlete? Try Cal Ripken, who was a 2007 enshrinee in baseball's Hall of Fame. Ripken, who, in 1995, broke Lou Gehrig's record for consecutive games played, played in 2,632 games in a row before finally taking a day off in 1998. He began his streak in 1982.

"I am proud of what I did and I thought it was my job to be out there every day," Ripken said. "But comparing what I did to what Jim Marshall did and what Brett Favre has done are two different things. That game is just so much more physically demanding."

Amazingly, Marshall did all that as a relatively skinny player. At 235 pounds, Marshall never had any qualms about playing against men who were 40, 50, or 60 pounds heavier. His durability amazed Bud Grant, who described him to *Sports Illustrated* as a "physiological impossibility. He just doesn't rip, bust, or tear."

That's not to say that Marshall didn't have health problems. He walked out of the hospital with pneumonia in order to keep

Jim Marshall played in an astounding 282 consecutive games on the defensive line for the Vikings and was a steady, stoic leader on the famed Purple People Eaters squad.

on playing. He was also very active in risky off-the-field activities, including sky diving, snowmobiling, and scuba diving. Marshall was a key cog in the Purple People Eaters. He got down and dirty in the trenches and he often was the one directing traffic before the snap of the ball. His all-around play—

TRIVIA

On what date was Minnesota awarded an NFL franchise?

Find the answers on pages 193–194.

excelling against the run and rushing the passer—would make him a consistent All-Pro in today's game, in which defensive ends are almost always judged on their pass-rush ability.

During the early part of Marshall's career, the league didn't count sacks or quarterback hurries, although he is currently credited with 127 sacks. The NFL didn't count sacks as an official statistic until 1982 and a quarterback trap behind the line of scrimmage didn't even have a name until Deacon Jones of the Rams came up with the imaginative word in the mid-1960s. If the "sack" had been around for the whole of Marshall's career, it's conceivable that he might have had more than current NFL career leader Bruce Smith, who finished his 18-year career with an even 200 sacks.

Marshall was also a remarkable leader. That's only natural for a man who was with the Vikings since their inception and played 19 years. (He played with Cleveland in 1960 before being traded to the expansion Vikings.) He wasn't always a holler guy, but when he spoke, his teammates listened. He did things the right way, came to play every day, and never asked for any relief.

Marshall has never been one to seek personal glory or lament that he is not in the Hall of Fame. Instead, his pride comes from what he did as part of the Vikings front four along with Alan Page, Carl Eller, and Gary Larsen.

"At our peak," he said, "we changed the game. Rules were passed to help teams adjust to us. The new holding rules, the outlawing of the head slap—that was because of the things we did. We were like a SWAT team, a strike task force because we were quick and agile. Apart, we were entirely different, but put us together and we clicked. It got to the point where I knew what the others were going to do the moment they started it. It was just understood."

Today that's called chemistry. In the 1960s and '70s, it was called teamwork.

For all the great plays and games that Marshall had, he is best remembered for a humorous mistake he made on October 25, 1964. In that game, at San Francisco's ancient Kezar Stadium, Eller punished San Francisco's Billy Kilmer with a big shot and the ball squirted loose.

Marshall, hustling the whole way, picked it up and started galloping at full speed toward the goal line. Unfortunately, he had gotten turned around chasing Kilmer's fumble and ran toward the Vikings' end zone and not the 49ers'. The play, immortalized by NFL Films, ended with Marshall running 66 yards and crossing the goal line and tossing the ball into the stands in celebration.

But instead of being surrounded by his teammates, San Francisco center Bruce Bosley came up to him, patted him on the shoulder pads, and thanked him. It was only then that Marshall realized he had not scored a touchdown for the Vikings. Instead, he had given the 49ers a safety.

"I was so intent on picking the ball up and doing something with it that I wasn't even aware of what I had done until the ball had been whistled dead," Marshall recalled. "It was the perfect example of a young player using energy without thinking."

Interestingly, Eller and Marshall had combined to force a fumble on the previous series. Just 44 seconds earlier, Marshall knocked the ball from quarterback George Mira's grasp. Eller scooped up the football and returned it 45 yards for the first and only touchdown of his career.

Marshall's memorable gaffe did no damage, as the Vikings came away with a 27–22 victory.

NOT JUST AN ORDINARY JOE

The Vikings under Bud Grant had an image of being a conservative and well-disciplined team. This was partially true. They didn't take a lot of penalties and there were not a lot of off-the-field problems—especially compared to Vikings teams of the mid-1980s and beyond.

But as far as being conservative on the field, that was not the case. Grant might have been relatively expressionless on the sideline, but he was not a three-yards-and-a-cloud-of-dust kind of coach. He altered his game plan to meet his players' talents—and not the other way around.

When Grant took over in 1967, the Vikings were in the midst of a transition. They had traded Fran Tarkenton to the New York Giants and had brought in a relatively unknown quarterback from the Canadian Football League named Joe Kapp.

Kapp was not a classic passer like John Unitas, Bart Starr, John Brodie, or any of the top quarterbacks of the era. There was nothing glamorous about Kapp. He was a brutally tough man with a personality more befitting of a linebacker than a quarterback.

"You won't ever see me running out of bounds," Kapp explained at the time. "That just isn't what I'm about. If you want contact, I'll give it to you."

Kapp didn't look at a game as gentlemanly competition between two sides looking for honorable victory. Instead, to him it was as simple as a street fight.

"Maybe it's my heritage or maybe it's just inside me," said Kapp. "I just know I am not going to back down. I did it once when I was in the seventh grade and I never backed down again. If you wanted to tangle, I was ready."

It was with that personality in mind that Grant and Vikings General Manager Jim Finks decided to make Kapp their quarterback. He had the look of a street fighter—with perhaps one or two drinks in him—but he was a very effective leader even if his passes often had the look of a wounded duck.

Kapp had been a winning quarterback with the British Columbia Lions and his first opportunity to play in the NFL came as the Vikings were getting beaten up badly by the Los Angeles Rams. Ron VanderKelen and Bob Berry had both gotten hammered by the Rams defense, so Grant had no choice but to give Kapp his baptism against a fearsome Los Angeles pass rush.

BRUSHING ASIDE THE SUPER BOWL EDICT

You've heard it so many times that it is accepted as gospel. In order to be considered one of the greats of all time, a quarterback must win the big one. He must bring home a Super Bowl title.

After all, a quarterback's primary job is to lead his team. Lead his team down the field in a clutch situation and put points on the board when the game is on the line. It's what is expected in the regular season and it is demanded in the postseason.

Don't win a Super Bowl and a player's legacy is tainted.

Ridiculous. It wasn't true for Dan Marino or Dan Fouts. And it certainly was not the case for Fran Tarkenton. Those are just a few of the great quarterbacks never to win the big one. Add in John Brodie, Roman Gabriel, Jim Kelly, Sonny Jurgensen, and Warren Moon as great quarterbacks who never won the Super Bowl. Because they don't have a ring, does that mean their career is demeaned or diminished?

Is Trent Dilfer on some higher plain because he was behind center for a Baltimore Ravens team that obliterated the Giants in Super Bowl XXXV? Does Brad Johnson have a "winning gene" because he was the quarterback for the Bucs when they hammered Oakland 48–21 in Super Bowl XXXVII?

Of course not. Nothing against Joe Montana, Tom Brady, Terry Bradshaw, or Steve Young, but Marino, Fouts, and Tarkenton are among the best quarterbacks to play the game. Tarkenton might not have been at his best in the big game, but he led an expansion team in the first part of his career and an ordinary New York Giants team in the second part. During the third act of his career, he led the Vikings to three Super Bowl appearances.

He didn't win those games, but opposing defenses knew that if Fran Tarkenton had the ball in the late stages of the fourth quarter, it was going to be life-or-death to hold on.

"He was the one guy I did not want to see on the other side of the line of scrimmage," said Hall of Fame defensive end Deacon Jones. "He was fast, elusive, quick, and all of that. I got him a few times, but you were just exhausted after playing against him."

Jones is credited with coining the term "sack." He was an All-NFL performer for five straight years and played the game to destroy quarterbacks.

Hall of Fame tight end and head coach Mike Ditka played against Tarkenton throughout his career, coached against Marino, and now, as a TV analyst, is among the most knowledgeable observers of football out there.

"All I ever hear about is Montana and Young and Brady," Ditka said. "Nothing against them. They all are great quarterbacks. But are you trying to tell me that they were better than Tarkenton or Marino simply because those guys don't have a ring? That's ridiculous.

"I'll tell you what. You can have those Super Bowl winners and leave me with Marino or Tarkenton. I'm happy with that and I'll beat you. No doubt in my mind. Marino could make every throw in the book and Tarkenton could do it all. No limitations at all. None."

Tarkenton drove defenses wild with his quick feet and even quicker decisions on the move. Ditka's old teammate, former Bears linebacker Doug Buffone, spent much of his career chasing him around or trying to cover his receivers.

"You were never so tired after a game as when you were playing against Tarkenton," Buffone said. "He was so quick you couldn't catch him. Normally with a pocket passer, you have to cover a back or tight end two or three seconds before he gets rid of the ball. But with Tarkenton, you had to cover a guy, I don't know, five seconds or more. That's 'cause he was running around and you could never catch him."

By buying an extraordinary amount of time, Tarkenton didn't necessarily have to zip the ball to his receiver. "He would be running around back there and you didn't know whether to stay with your guy or go after Tarkenton," Buffone said. "Enough time goes by and you go after him. He sees an open running back and he shot puts the ball over your head and he's got another completion. It was so frustrating.

"I remember I intercepted him once. It was just a straight drop back and he got rid of the ball quickly from the pocket. I was there and I made the play. But if he was running around, it was impossible to intercept those passes."

Kapp came into the game breathing fire, snapping off epithets to the Rams, and challenging them. That only served to further anger the Rams and big tackle Roger Brown dropped Kapp and landed on top of him. Kapp chided him for bad breath and then took more of a beating.

The 1967 season turned out to be one step forward followed by two steps back for Kapp. He had shown enough to make his presence felt and he knew he had an opportunity to establish himself as the number one quarterback if he could perform well in the season finale against the Lions. However, Detroit defensive tackle Alex Karras was at the top of his game and prevented Kapp from doing anything. Kapp threw three interceptions to All-Pro cornerback Lem Barney, and that showing in a 14–3 loss forced GM Jim Finks and Grant to bring in Gary Cuozzo as competition. Cuozzo had backed up John Unitas and was an accurate passer who knew how to read defenses.

Injuries kept Cuozzo from making a run at the job, and Kapp was much better in his second year in the NFL. Kapp's numbers were not overly impressive—he completed 129 of 248 passes for 1,695 yards with 10 touchdowns and 17 interceptions. He also ran for 269 yards and three touchdowns, averaging 5.4 yards per attempt. He often finished those runs by inflicting the blow like a fullback, rather than absorbing it.

The Vikings won the division title and were matched with the powerful Baltimore Colts in the playoffs. Minnesota dropped a 24–14 decision to the team that lost Super Bowl III to the Jets, but had competed on nearly even terms with the Colts. They had been done in by mistakes, and one was a Kapp fumble that was grabbed by Colts linebacker Mike Curtis, who returned it 60 yards for a touchdown.

Kapp built off that game to prepare for the 1969 season, and it was one that the Vikings would never forget. The defense was led by the front four of Jim Marshall, Carl Eller, Gary Larsen, and Alan Page and they were a devastating unit. And not just on Sundays. Kapp felt their wrath during the week in practice and he figured if he could survive that group, handling his business in a game would not be a problem.

Kapp's teammates believed in him as well. Not because of any great talent or because of any personal glory, but because he played every down as if it were his last with a will to win that few had seen. Kapp knew he didn't have great physical gifts, but he knew how to battle.

"I figured I was playing with the best group of football players in the world and there was one area that I could beat them in: desire," Kapp explained to *Sports Illustrated* in a brilliant series written in 1970. "I can want to win more than anybody in the world and I do. Not for the fans, not for the press, and not for the money. For personal pride. Playing the best you can and getting everything out of your abilities. That's what I try to impress on my teammates."

The 1969 season started with an ignominious 24–23 defeat to an ordinary New York Giants team that would not reach the .500 mark. But the next week, the Vikings destroyed the Colts 52–14 as the team came together in a huge way to exact a bit of revenge on the team that had eliminated them the year before. Kapp tied an NFL record in the game with seven touchdown passes, and after the game reporters crowded around him to get his take on the beating administered to the Colts and to make him a star.

Kapp would have none of it. In his mind, playing quarterback was just another position on the team.

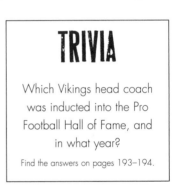

TRIVIA

Which Vikings head coach was inducted into the Pro Football Hall of Fame, and in what year?

Find the answers on pages 193–194.

The only thing he wanted credit for was helping to instill some winning spirit in the team. The Vikings would reel off 12 straight wins before dropping their meaningless season finale against the Falcons.

The Vikings were so team-oriented that a slogan emerged: "40 for 60." It included the special teams, which were clearly the best in the NFL and superbly coached by Grant. Everybody on the team contributed to the winning streak including the backups. Grant had a full-fledged locomotive of a team on his hands and Kapp was a huge part of it.

In the playoffs, the Vikings played poorly but managed to overcome sloppy play to come back and beat the Rams 23–20. That set up the last NFL championship game ever played that was not the final game of the season. The 1969 season was the last year that the AFL and the NFL played as separate leagues. The Vikings would play for the NFL title against a Cleveland Browns team that had beaten the Cowboys, while the Chiefs would meet the Raiders for the AFL crown.

The Vikings were fully confident that they would handle Cleveland. They had beaten the Browns 51–3 midway through the season. They knew Cleveland was better than that, but the Vikings fully realized that if they played their best game they would win the NFL championship game.

Early in the game, Kapp and fullback Bill Brown missed connections on a handoff and Kapp found himself with the ball in his

Joe Kapp brought a blue-collar identity to the powerful team from Minnesota.

hands. He went on instinct and barged straight ahead, plowing between defensive linemen Walter Johnson and Mike Howell and leaving them on the ground. Kapp got to the end zone and his teammates mobbed him.

That play was good, but perhaps the most memorable play of Kapp's career came a bit later. He had called a pass play to Gene Washington, but the wide receiver was double covered and John Henderson wasn't open on the other side of the field. So Kapp took off around right end.

Cleveland's All-Pro linebacker Jim Houston was right in front of him. Kapp could easily have gone to the sidelines but that was never his style and it wouldn't be on this day. Instead, he barreled full steam into Houston, leaping just before impact. Kapp went flying and did a complete flip in the air. Houston went down—and out.

Kapp's knee had hit Houston right on the point of the chin and knocked him cold. That play infused the Vikings and sapped the Browns. The Vikings had the NFL title as a result of their 27–7 victory.

The atmosphere in the locker room was decidedly businesslike. They were not celebrating the win with much fervor because they were already looking forward to the Super Bowl and a date with the Kansas City Chiefs.

The Vikings had quite a bit of pressure on them to recapture the NFL's glory. The Colts had been defeated 16–7 by the New York Jets and that game had given the AFL credibility. The Chiefs knew they would gain even more of it for themselves and their AFL brethren if they could take care of the powerful Vikings. Minnesota wanted to show the NFL's loss the year before was nothing but a fluke.

Kapp sensed that something was wrong with his team immediately after the win over the Browns. "We squirted a few bottles of champagne around the locker room and then the mood turned businesslike," Kapp said. "We were a group of proud and happy warriors, but all of a sudden it was like it was wrong to celebrate the NFL championship. The talk and attention immediately turned to the Super Bowl. That was a major mistake. We should have partied and celebrated."

The Vikings were installed as 13-point favorites over the Chiefs, but Kansas City was big, strong, and talented. As the Vikings prepared for the game, Kapp and Cuozzo sensed that their team was not operating at its peak and the players were flat.

"I should have been able to do something about it," Kapp explained. "I should have been able to diagnose the problem and figure out what was wrong. I just didn't have the experience or sense for the moment. But never take anything away from them. They played one of the greatest games in modern pro football history and we didn't. They won the game and they deserved to."

The score was 23–7 and it really wasn't that close. The Chiefs dominated physically and late in the fourth quarter, Kansas City defensive lineman Aaron Brown caught Kapp from behind and slammed him to the ground on his shoulder. The pain knocked Kapp out and when he came to a few minutes later, he found Cuozzo in the huddle. "Was I glad to see him," Kapp recalled.

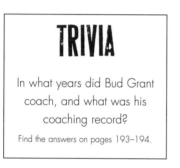

TRIVIA

In what years did Bud Grant coach, and what was his coaching record?

Find the answers on pages 193–194.

Kapp had torn several key ligaments and muscles and suffered a shoulder separation. The Chiefs finished their victory and the Vikings' brilliant season ended in defeat.

However, there was nothing for Kapp or his teammates to be ashamed of. They had enjoyed a great season, but just could not close the deal. It was a feeling that Vikings fans would become familiar with.

Kapp, however, would not. He engaged the Vikings in a nasty contract holdout and was later traded to the Boston Patriots. The Vikings finished the season with a 12–2 record in the regular season, but dropped their playoff game at home against the underdog San Francisco 49ers. Kapp struggled in his new environment and his career was soon over.

However, the quarterback known as "the Man of Machismo" played the game with an élan that was not soon forgotten, endearing himself to the Vikings' loyal fan base.

BRINGING FEAR TO A NEW LEVEL

Few players have the ability to inspire fear in those on the other side of the line of scrimmage. In the 1950s, the Eagles had Chuck "Concrete Charlie" Bednarik, a two-way player who became infamous for his tackle of Giants running back Frank Gifford that knocked the future TV analyst out of action for a full season.

In the 1960s, Bears middle linebacker Dick Butkus was the picture of aggression, running full force toward ball carriers in an effort to destroy them—not tackle them.

In the 1970s, defensive tackle Joe Greene led the Steelers to four Super Bowl titles. He was an outstanding player and a skilled leader, but he also played with mayhem in his heart that terrified opposing players.

In the 1980s, Lawrence Taylor became the most feared player in football because he propelled himself like a rocket around the field in an effort to inflict pain on quarterbacks and running backs. In one memorable moment in a 1985 Monday night game, he snapped Washington quarterback Joe Theismann's leg as if it were a Thanksgiving wishbone.

The Vikings had their own destroyer in the mid-1980s who was about to become as much of a legend as Bednarik, Butkus, Greene, and Taylor.

Keith Millard was a large and nasty defensive tackle who took grown men and made them fear for their safety when he was at the height of his power.

If you think we are going a bit too far, ask former 49ers All-Pro guard Jesse Sapolu, who was forced to battle Millard four times from 1986 through the end of the 1988 postseason.

In the 1988 playoffs, the 49ers punished the Vikings 34–9 in the divisional playoff game to earn a spot in the NFC championship game in Chicago under freezing winter conditions against Mike Ditka's Bears.

Chicago was expected to dominate the game. Few thought the 49ers could hold up under the winter conditions. But these 49ers were a superb team who were not about to expire simply because they were playing in Bear weather. Joe Montana and Jerry Rice

THE MENTAL GAME

Fran Tarkenton knew early on that he could create headaches for opposing defenses. His ability to scramble away from pressure and then make a play on the run made his receivers and running backs far more productive than they would have been without him.

Tarkenton could throw from the pocket and clearly did that well. But opposing coaches and defensive coordinators lost control when Tarkenton got outside the pocket.

"He was always a headache for us," said longtime NFL head coach Chuck Knox, whose Los Angeles Ram teams regularly battled with the Vikings from 1973 through 1977. "He had the ability to turn the game upside down when he got outside the pocket and was scrambling. They had very disciplined linemen who would rarely get called for holding. You need that when you have a quarterback who holds on to the ball that long."

Tarkenton not only used his ability to escape to stay out of harm's way and make a play, he also designed scrambles just to confuse defenses. He would regularly run in one direction and then make a play on the opposite side of the field when the defense was drawn to him.

A generation knows Ahmad Rashad as a sportscaster and television personality. He was especially prominent in the 1990s, when the Chicago Bulls were winning NBA championships, because he was a close friend of Michael Jordan's. If you wanted to know what Jordan's inner circle was like, you listened to Rashad.

Many of those watching him either had no idea or very limited recollections of Ahmad Rashad as a receiver with the Vikings. Drafted by the St. Louis Cardinals in 1972 when he went by the name of Bobby Moore, he was traded to the Buffalo Bills in 1974 and then to the Vikings two years later.

Rashad enjoyed great success with the Vikings, going to the Pro Bowl four straight years from 1978–81. Rashad had a great rapport on the field with Tarkenton until the quarterback retired after the 1978 season, and Rashad knew how Tarkenton liked to set up opposing defenses.

"Fran would a call a play in the huddle," Rashad recalled. "Maybe it was a deep pass or perhaps there was a combination of receivers involved.

Then he'd pull me aside and do what we had talked about privately earlier in the week.

"Here's what I'm talking about. He'd call one play that had three receivers on the right side. I'd be on the left. He would scramble to the right and I would be standing on the left side of the line of scrimmage, basically all by myself."

That was Tarkenton's design. He tried to suck in the defense and then do the opposite. "Everybody is thinking that Fran is improvising and going off on his own. But the truth was that it was all planned. A planned scramble. He ran back to the left and found me all alone and tossed me a three-yard pass. Nobody was near me so I could run for 30 yards."

Tarkenton would continue to do that until the defense adjusted—and then he would change his game plan once again.

had their way with the Chicago defense and rolled to a surprisingly easy 28–3 win.

In the locker room, the 49ers were frozen but happy. Sapolu was asked about his matchup with future Hall of Famer Dan Hampton, who was nearing the end of a brilliant career.

Sapolu sat in front of his locker collecting his thoughts. "I don't mean any disrespect to Dan Hampton, but I was not worried about this matchup," Sapolu explained. "He's a great player who does everything well. But last week I had to block Keith Millard. Do you think anything would bother me after going up against him? That guy's just a monster. He's not from this world. So going up against a great player the following week is not a tough assignment.

"Even here in this weather, going up against that great defense of Chicago's, from my perspective, it didn't compare to going up against Millard. Even though we were at home and won the game by what—more than three touchdowns—that was painful. He is strong, mean, and nasty. Every play was a war."

Millard had incredible quickness to go with his mean streak and had eight sacks in 1988. The next year was his masterpiece, finishing the season with 18 sacks from the middle of the defensive line and combining with teammate Chris Doleman for 39 sacks. Doleman was very fast and skilled on his own, but the presence of Millard allowed him to erupt all over the league.

Millard was recognized as the league's defensive MVP for his record-setting performance. Despite his ability to dominate a game and intimidate opponents, Millard had several off-the-field problems, most of them dealing with driving. A 1990 DUI arrest was later reduced to reckless driving, but it showed that Millard had lifestyle issues that were a concern for the team.

His brilliant career came apart at the seams after he was on the receiving end of a cut block from Tampa Bay offensive lineman Paul Gruber.

The Vikings were hosting the Bucs in Week 4 of the 1990 season and Millard was wreaking havoc once again. He had Gruber beaten and was on his way to sacking Bucs quarterback Vinny Testaverde. Millard sensed that Gruber would throw himself at his legs, so he jumped in an effort to avoid the hit. He was unable to do so.

"It's still clear to me," said Millard. "I had Gruber beat and he started to cut me. I jumped to avoid it, but it just happened. I knew right then it was over immediately."

Millard explained that the prime of his career was over because of the severity of the ACL injury. He would rehab the injury and keep on trying to show that he could play until 1993, but he was a shell of his former self.

Millard went into a major depression at his realization that he could no longer play up to his standards. The Vikings had no other choice but to move on. John Randle took the opportunity and ran with it. No, he wasn't quite as good as Millard, but he was an impact player who became one of the team leaders.

"I saw everything I was doing go up in smoke," Millard said. "I felt like I lost my identity. I was a Viking ... I was a sack leader, and then it was over. It was difficult to take."

But Millard battled through his depression and moved on. He stayed with football and is a successful NFL assistant coach. He coached the defensive line of the Oakland Raiders in 2005 and 2006 and while Oakland had the worst record in the league, the defense was widely respected. Millard is considered a coach on the rise in the NFL; a major turnaround for a great player whose days on the field ended so painfully. He appears to be past his off-the-field issues as well and it's not inconceivable that Millard may one day be a head-coaching candidate in the NFL.

CRIS CARTER: THE HANDS OF AN ARTIST

He was the best receiver to wear a Vikings uniform and one of the best ever to play the game.

However, it didn't start out that way for Cris Carter. As a young receiver for the Eagles and Buddy Ryan, Carter considered himself an invincible player who could go out and party all week and do his job on Sunday. Dedication and conditioning—two factors he would be known for throughout his tenure in Minnesota—were non-issues in Philadelphia.

"When I was in Philadelphia, we used to cash our paychecks after practice and go to Atlantic City," he told a group of NFL rookies in 2005 who were preparing for life in the fish bowl. "We would party and gamble all night. We'd stay there and drive back to Philadelphia in the morning. We'd sleep in the parking lot and tell the security guards to wake us up when everyone else got there.

"You guys don't have the market cornered on dumb stuff. It's unbelievable all the dumb stuff I did."

Carter's lack of dedication didn't show on the field, as he caught 45 passes for 605 yards with a whopping 11 touchdowns in 1989. But Ryan was not impressed because he believed Carter was more interested in partying, alcohol, and drugs than he was in helping the Eagles win football games. In a move that shocked those outside Philadelphia, Ryan cut the productive Carter.

"Buddy Ryan told me he couldn't depend on me," Carter said. "He didn't know if I would flunk a drug test. He didn't know what I might do."

The move was the seminal moment in Carter's life and career. He did not like what he saw when he looked in the mirror.

"After I got cut, I was driving across the Walt Whitman Bridge," Carter said. "I had to call my wife and tell her I got cut. She was at home, pregnant with our first son. She had just graduated college and turned down a job offer to come to Philadelphia with me."

The sure-handed Cris Carter points skyward after catching one of his three touchdown receptions in the Vikings' 39–28 win over the Colts in the final game of the 1997 regular season.

The devastated Carter realized his misfortune was all of his own doing. He vowed to clean himself up and hasn't had a drink since September 1990.

A receiver who can dominate in the red zone like Carter doesn't stay unemployed very long. The Vikings called the next day to sign Carter and they picked up a bona fide all-time great.

Carter had excellent leaping ability and great athleticism, but lacked the great stopwatch speed that personnel people look for when scouting receivers. Once Carter got to Minnesota, he became a tireless worker who did everything he could to get better on an everyday basis. Combining his physical gifts with that relentless attitude helped turn Carter into one of the NFL's brightest stars.

During the 1994 season, Carter caught a league record 122 passes. He matched that total the following year, but Detroit's Herman Moore edged past his record with 123 receptions. Seven years after that, virtuoso Colts receiver Marvin Harrison caught 143 passes to become the record holder.

Carter played in an era when San Francisco's Jerry Rice dominated and the Cowboys' Michael Irvin also made headlines. As a result, Carter was one of the league's most unappreciated superstars during the early part of his Minnesota career. However, all of his talents were cherished by head coach Dennis Green.

"I think Cris is more acrobatic and will make more difficult catches than those other guys," Green said. "You see a pass that you think he has no chance to catch because it's too high or will go out of bounds and then he does something that you don't believe. He'll dive for a ball and make a catch by scooping it or he will keep the tips of his toes in bounds while reaching over the barrier to make a catch. Nobody else can do it like Cris."

Carter excelled at all aspects of the game, but it was his hands that made him special. Carter regularly bathed his best assets in paraffin and oil to soothe and relax them. He took care of them and pampered them during the week—and they took care of him on Sundays.

The diving catch? Nobody did it better than Carter. But that's just the start. Fingertip catches. Back-of-the-ball catches.

TRIVIA

What is Bud Grant's
real first name?

Find the answers on pages 193–194.

One-handed diving catches. He was dominant in the red zone where he used his 6'3", 220-pound frame and ability to catch anything he could get his hands on to his advantage.

His trademark was the sideline catch, where he stretched like a contortionist, his entire body out of bounds except for his tiptoeing feet. Nobody made those catches as often or as well as Carter.

The addition of Warren Moon to the Vikings lineup in 1994 may have provided the impetus Carter needed to go from star player to one of the league's all-time greats at the position. "Warren has meant a great deal to me," Carter said during the middle of the '94 season. "He's so professional and such an accurate passer. The trade we made to get him makes it a lot easier to do my job."

Carter, whose brother Butch played in the NBA for six seasons, used a lot of basketball skills while on the football field. His athleticism, coordination, and ability to screen defensive backs from the ball were taken from his basketball instincts.

"You can tell a lot about a football player by the way he plays basketball," said Bud Grant, who played pro football and in the NBA during his younger years. "Some guys worry about catching the ball but Cris is beyond that. If Cris got a hand or a finger on it, you knew he was going to bring it in. He was concerned about what he would do before he caught the ball and after he caught it, but he didn't have to worry about catching it because he was so instinctive in that area."

As Carter established himself as one of the team's brightest stars, he took on more and more of a leadership role. Carter was not hesitant to tell the coaching staff if he thought the wrong play was called or call out another player for making a mistake. Carter's emotional nature may have rubbed some of his teammates the wrong way, but it was an honest reaction that he refused to keep bottled up.

"I'm an emotional guy and when I get upset on the football field I have a reason," Carter said. "It was never about getting me the football more. If the tight end read the defense incorrectly, I'm all over the tight end. If the offensive coordinator calls a play that we didn't practice during the week, I'm questioning him on the sideline."

Carter knew that his propensity for calling players and coaches out left him vulnerable if he didn't continue to perform at a high level. That provided Carter with even more motivation to stay on top of his game.

"I can stay in the position I'm in only if I play at a high level," he said. "If I don't, then I lose my voice in the locker room."

Carter's demanding attitude was forged by Ryan's decision to part company with him in Philadelphia. By showing his teammates "tough love" on a consistent basis, he was trying to force them to do their best.

"My whole philosophy is it's not okay to make a mental mistake," Carter said. "I know if a guy is hanging out nightclubbing because he is hurting in the fourth quarter. When that's the case I'm going to have something to say to him because the veterans are depending on him. My whole attitude, performance, and play is designed to get the most out of everyone on the team."

Carter played for the Vikings from 1990 through the 2001 season and finished his NFL career by playing five games for the Dolphins in 2002. He caught 1,101 passes during his career for 13,899 yards and 130 touchdowns. That figure ranks second on the all-time list to Rice, who finished his career with 197 touchdowns.

Carter also made eight straight Pro Bowls, beginning with the 1993 season. During that eight-year run, Carter averaged 97.4 catches, 1,182 yards, and 11.3 touchdowns. Carter was proud of his overall numbers, but they were never his focus. "The one thing I wanted people to say about my career is that I was dependable," Carter said.

His numbers, his dedication, and his lesson learned proved that he was just that.

THINGS TO SAVOR

CALL HIM BOOM-BOOM, CALL HIM OLD FOOTBALL FACE

The Vikings were a team of tough men in the late 1960s and '70s, nasty players who were happy to engage their opponents in physical battles.

The defense had the headliners—men like Jim Marshall, Carl Eller, Alan Page, and Wally Hilgenberg who would dole out punishment—but the offense was not a finesse group, either.

While Fran Tarkenton and receivers like Gene Washington, John Gilliam, and Ahmad Rashad made their share of eye-catching and beautiful plays, the Vikings offense was not a finesse offense. Make no mistake about it. When the Vikings inherited the throne from the Green Bay Packers as the best all-around team in the NFC, it wasn't because they were afraid to get physical.

Linemen like Ron Yary, Mick Tinglehoff, Grady Alderman, and Jim Vellone were solid and effective blockers who had a nasty edge. But they were not alone in their ability to batter and bruise.

The constant in the backfield was Bill "Boom-Boom" Brown, a battering ram of a fullback who took as much pleasure in delivering a bone-crunching block as he did in running the ball. With backfield mate Dave Osborn running next to him, the Vikings had a competent running game to go along with either Tarkenton or Joe Kapp's passing. Both were solid runners and receivers and Osborn could block, but Brown was clearly superior in that area. Osborn gave the same kind of effort as Brown, but Boom-Boom was as hard as a piece of cut granite and he pounded away first and asked questions later.

Because he looked like the quintessential 1950s and '60s football player, Brown's overall skills were often underestimated. Certainly that was the case when the Bears traded Brown to the Vikings following his rookie year in 1961. George Halas sent Brown to

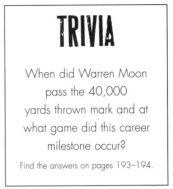

TRIVIA

When did Warren Moon pass the 40,000 yards thrown mark and at what game did this career milestone occur?

Find the answers on pages 193–194.

Minnesota in exchange for a fourth-round pick in the 1963 draft. That pick turned out to be Mike Reilly, an ordinary linebacker from Iowa who lasted five years with Chicago.

Halas, the godfather of professional football, knew Brown was a talent when he drafted him in the second round. However, Halas took leave of his senses after the Bears went 8–6 and finished three games behind the hated Packers in the NFL's Western Conference. He decided Brown was not the player he thought he was after seeing the rookie run for 81 yards on 22 carries that season.

Halas made other poor choices throughout his long tenure, but trading Brown for a fourth-round pick after his rookie season was one of his worst. Brown, an Illinois native, also graduated from the University of Illinois and had a strong following. He was a Papa Bear kind of player whose best attribute was his toughness. He had all the other skills, but Brown could take a player into the alley and make him sorry that he ever decided on football as a vocation.

Brown went on to play 13 more years for the Vikings, four of which ended with selections to the Pro Bowl. Brown—also known as "Old Football Face" by modern pundits—started to thrive as soon as he went to Minnesota.

He made his mark in 1963 with 445 yards and five touchdowns and his crunching style became his signature. However, he became one of the league's most effective players the following year. Brown ran for 866 yards and seven touchdowns and also caught 48 passes for 703 yards and nine touchdowns. In addition to becoming a scoring machine, Brown maintained his ability to bowl over linebackers with a single shoulder to the midsection.

Halas was sickened by Brown's success in Minnesota, knowing he could have been dominating for the Bears and not the Vikings.

"Hey, I could throw it too," said Brown, who completed two of three passes in his career. "But that rarely happened. The Vikings realized that I could get open on deep or short passes, so we tried it and it worked."

Brown caught 286 passes for 3,183 yards with 23 touchdowns in his career. As a runner, he pounded out 5,838 yards and reached the end zone 52 times while averaging 3.5 yards per carry. They don't keep stats on blocking, but Brown left hundreds of linebackers and defensive backs in his wake. He was the game's ultimate lead blocker.

Brown, of course, played his career while the Vikings played their home games at wide open Metropolitan Stadium. Despite the brutally cold weather and strong winds, Brown thrived in that environment.

"I loved playing at the Met," Brown said. "It was always freezing up there, but the field was in great shape. The only time we had problems was in the middle of a snowstorm or heavy downpour. The ground would tear up under your feet in those situations."

Brown was with the Vikings when they got to their first three Super Bowls. Their losses to the Chiefs, Dolphins, and Steelers still burn in Brown's memory.

"Winning the Super Bowl was something we should have done," said Brown. "You get three chances to do it and you really should have won one of them. I'm very competitive and to go 0–3 in those games still hurts."

But the pain of those losses doesn't compare to the joy he felt playing with one of the dominant teams in that era. The Vikings were consistent and quite close as a team and Brown believes that the players on the field today don't experience anywhere near the closeness that he and his teammates felt while they were dominating the NFL and then the NFC.

"We played well together and we were a very close-knit group," Brown said. "We played together for a very long time and that's something you don't see today because of free agency. Teams have a hard time keeping their players together. That's a bad thing because it takes time to learn how your teammates do things. If players don't mesh together right away—no matter how talented they are—they move on."

Toughness, togetherness, and tenacity were three of the key ingredients for the Vikings throughout Brown's career. Those elements were never in doubt during his run. The same cannot be said once he retired from the game. Football—and the Vikings— have been poorer without Boom-Boom and his unforgettable presence on the field and in the locker room.

PURPLE PEOPLE EATERS: LET'S MEET AT THE QUARTERBACK

The great Vikings teams of the 1960s and '70s had many elements. A couple of memorable quarterbacks in Fran Tarkenton and Joe Kapp. A running game that could pound it with Bill Brown and Dave Osborn or make huge plays with Chuck Foreman. Receivers who could take it the distance, such as Sammy White and Gene Washington and a slew of smart and punishing linebackers like Roy Winston and Lonnie Warwick. Even place-kicker Fred Cox sticks out in the memory bank, with his square-toed shoe and straight-ahead style. Nothing fancy, but very effective.

However, the greatest and most devastating talent on the team came from its powerful pass rush. Given the name the "Purple People Eaters" by headline writers, the group included defensive ends Jim Marshall and Carl Eller along with defensive tackles Alan Page and Gary Larsen terrorized backfields from 1967 through 1974. Marshall, Eller, and Page continued to produce through the 1978 season along with defensive tackle Doug Sutherland after Larsen's playing days were over.

They never really liked that garish nickname or the attending publicity that went with it. They didn't mind being call the Purple Gang, but any other moniker rubbed them the wrong way. This was about as professional a group as the game has ever seen. Befitting the personality of their head coach, Bud Grant, there were no celebrations after a sack, a tackle, a forced fumble, or an interception. There was nothing for them to celebrate because they were merely doing their job.

They did have a credo, however. Nearly every time they broke the huddle, they told each other to "meet at the quarterback."

The Purple Gang ranks with the best front fours the game has ever seen. They compare favorably with the Rams' Fearsome Foursome and Pittsburgh's Steel Curtain.

Alan Page was a cornerstone of the Vikings' Purple People Eaters. His speed and explosiveness from the defensive tackle position made it nearly impossible for opposing linemen to slow him down.

As good as they were at rushing the passer, they may have been even better against the run. Minnesota gave up only two rushing touchdowns in 1971, equaling the NFL record. In 1970 and '71, Minnesota gave up an average of one touchdown per game. The Purple Gang led the team to 10 division titles in 11 years, but once the unit started fading into retirement, the Vikings took only two division titles in the next 13 years.

The unit did not do it with size and bulk, as Larsen was the heaviest at 255 pounds. They were quick, decisive, and skilled in all aspects of the game.

Marshall might be known as the guy who ran the wrong way after scooping up Billy Kilmer's fumble at Kezar Stadium in 1964, but he was a truly great player whose prolific career includes a league-record 282 consecutive starts, 270 coming in a Vikings uniform. He went to Pro Bowls following the 1968 and 1969 seasons and finished his career with 127 sacks.

Marshall's infamous play has never been forgotten despite the consistent excellence he displayed throughout the rest of his career. "I set an NFL record with 29 career fumble recoveries," Marshall said. "Nobody ever wants to talk about the other 28. Hey, we won that game anyway [27–22]."

Marshall came to the Vikings in a trade with Cleveland prior to their expansion season of 1961. The Vikings spent two draft choices to get Marshall, defensive tackle Paul Dickson, and four other players.

Eller was an All-American for the Minnesota Golden Gophers and was a first-round draft pick in 1964. Vikings coach Norm Van Brocklin was skeptical about rookies—but Eller made him change his mind. He was a starter right away and played in 225 games and became the team's all-time leader with 130 sacks.

Page was drafted out of Notre Dame in 1967 and had monstrous talent. Not only was he strong and agile when it came to stopping the run, Page was quick, smart, and mean with his pass rush. Page was often considered the best defensive player in the league in the early 1970s and won the Associated Press MVP in 1971. He had 108 sacks in a Vikings uniform before getting traded to Chicago in 1978.

Larsen was the stay-at-home tackle who rarely joined his fellow linemen in the pass rush. However, few could equal him when it came to stopping the interior run. He was able to tie up blockers, get penetration, and make plays. After Larsen's career came to an end, Doug Sutherland filled his spot on the Vikings defensive line.

While there was no shortage of physical talent, the group had great internal communication. The experience of playing together gave the group the ability to read each other's body language so they would know what their partners were doing.

"When you play together like we have, you get a lot of confidence in each other," Marshall told *Sports Illustrated* in 1969. "I know what Page is going to do and I know what [middle linebacker] Lonnie Warwick is going to do and I react instinctively.

"Some of the stunts are planned. Maybe Page and I will decide on the stunt and let the linebackers know what we are going to do. But sometimes we'll stunt because the blocking opens up, and when we do that we have to depend on our instinctive reactions."

Those reactions were superb, as the Vikings almost always had the edge in quickness and athleticism on their opponents. Take Eller, for example. At 6'5" and 250 pounds, Eller had a great first step that left opposing blockers reaching for air. He was an All-Pro five times, including four straight years, from 1968–71. Eller was like a shark in that the moment he sensed a weakness in an opposing tackle, he would turn up his motor even higher and wreak more havoc. Eller holds the Vikings team record for sacks with 130, and once recorded sacks in eight straight games.

Page was one of three Vikings—along with Fran Tarkenton and Randall Cunningham—to win the league's MVP award. He won the NFC defensive player of the year award four times and was exceptional at making momentum-changing plays. He recovered 23 fumbles during his career and also blocked an amazing 28 kicks. Page used his intelligence to set up opposing blockers with moves and counter-moves that allowed him to make big plays at key moments. Page played 15 seasons—11 with the Vikings and the last four with the Bears. He was incredibly durable, never missing a game in his career. He played in all 218 games for which he was eligible.

BEARS, LIONS SIMPLY INADEQUATE AT QUARTERBACK POSITION

The Vikings have been around since 1961, while the division rival Bears and Lions have been in business much longer. The Bears are one of the league's original franchises, while the Lions came into existence in 1934.

Despite both teams' longevity, neither team comes close to matching the Vikings in productivity at the quarterback position.

In an era when great quarterbacks have been plentiful, the Bears' all-time leader in passing yardage is Sid Luckman with 14,686 yards. Luckman is in the Hall of Fame and was an undeniably great and effective player. However, Luckman started his career in 1939 and retired in 1950. Despite the subsequent 57 seasons since Luckman wore a Bears uniform, he is still more than 3,000 yards ahead of Jim Harbaugh, who stands in second place with 11,567 yards.

It's a similar story in Detroit. Lions quarterback Bobby Layne was a great clutch performer and perhaps even more legendary for his antics off the field. He is the Lions' all-time passing leader with 15,710 yards. Layne played with the Lions from 1950 through 1958. He is 3,063 yards ahead of second-place Scott Mitchell.

The best quarterbacks the Bears have had since Luckman left have been Jim McMahon, Erik Kramer, Jim Miller, and Harbaugh. Vikings fans will remember that memorable game in which Harbaugh threw a fourth-quarter interception to Todd Scott that the strong safety returned for a touchdown late in the fourth quarter. That play gave the Vikings a 21–20 lead. Bears coach Mike Ditka ripped into Harbaugh on the sidelines without hesitation. As he read Harbaugh the riot act, television cameras caught the entire debacle. Ditka was fired at the end of the season and that game was where it all stated to unravel.

Detroit has had quarterbacks like Mitchell, Kramer, Greg Landry, Gary Danielson, Charlie Batch, Joey Harrington, and Eric Hipple.

Experience is supposed to be a telling factor in any business. But when it comes to finding quarterbacks, the Bears and Lions show that experience only means those teams have been in business a long time—with little to show for it at the game's most important position.

Now his focus is on helping the Minneapolis community. "It's all about giving back," Page said. "I don't know when children stop dreaming, but I do know when hope starts slipping away because I have seen it with my work with the community. We must educate our children—it's not an option. We must keep hope alive."

Page is clearly making the same mark off the field that he did when he was on the field, making life miserable for opposing quarterbacks and running backs.

MINNESOTA: LAND OF 10,000 QUARTERBACKS (WELL, AT LEAST 10)

There is the pain of four Super Bowl losses and the heartbreaking finish of the 1998 season. The consistency of the 1970s allowed this team to enter the national fray as one of the top franchises in the NFL.

There are certain teams that go beyond the appeal of being a local phenomenon. Teams like the Bears, Cowboys, Steelers, and Packers have national followings; the Vikings are in that group as well.

Their hard-hitting defense of the late 1960s and '70s with the colorful nickname of Purple People Eaters is one reason, but there's another major reason as well. The Vikings have had some of the game's greatest and most prolific quarterbacks.

The game's most important and glamorous position has yielded a bumper crop in Minnesota. Hall of Famer Fran Tarkenton started behind center for the team's first six seasons. Joe Kapp brought his machismo and fire to the team for three years and led the Vikings to their first Super Bowl. Tarkenton came back in a trade with the Giants and played brilliantly for seven more seasons.

After Tarkenton retired, the Vikings did not have to go through a transition period. Tommy "Tommy Gun" Kramer came in and played prolific football. He threw 83 touchdown passes in a four-year period during which the Vikings had just an average running attack. Kramer also earned the nickname of "Two-Minute Tommy" because he led a number of comebacks in the game's final minutes.

Viking quarterback Tommy Kramer was known for his last-minute comebacks and his ability to take a hit and come back for more—both on and off the field.

Kramer was a rough customer who had the ability to stand in the pocket and take the most vicious shots and still come back for more. Kramer has a quick release with first-rate arm strength. He was also known for the off-the-field exploits that made him a Vikings legend.

In 1987, Vikings general manager Mike Lynn revealed that Kramer underwent treatment for alcohol abuse. Kramer had a 28-day stay at a rehab facility, his second trip in five years.

Even non-stars like Wade Wilson, Rich Gannon, and Sean Salisbury played solid football at the position. None of those three had significant physical gifts, but they were all sharp passers who could read opposing defenses and make the right decision as to where to put the ball.

In 1994, Warren Moon resurrected his career with three memorable seasons in Minnesota. Moon's 1995 season was particularly

Warren
Moon

remarkable. At the age of 39, he completed 377 of 606 passes for 4,228 yards with 33 touchdowns and 14 interceptions.

Moon went into the Hall of Fame in 2006, having played the majority of his career for the Houston Oilers. But his 1995 season in Minnesota convinced all the doubters that Moon was not a product of any system and was truly a great quarterback. At his Hall of Fame induction speech, he remembered his years in Minnesota with fondness.

"I moved on to Minnesota, where Dennis Green didn't think I was done at the tender age of 38 years old," Moon said. "He gave me that chance to play football, along with Jeff Diamond, their general manager. I had a chance to be with Brian Billick and also Ray Sherman. We took that offense to some new heights."

Moon played at the start of an era when having an African American quarterback was no longer an issue in the NFL. Prior to that, very few black quarterbacks had been given opportunities to show what they could do in the pro ranks.

Moon realizes he became a torch bearer for black quarterbacks and has said his efforts, along with those of the players who preceded him and also those who played at the same time, have made life easier for quarterbacks like Michael Vick, Donovan McNabb, and Steve McNair.

"That is everything that guys before me like James Harris, Joe Gilliam, and Marlin Briscoe and for those who played with me like Randall Cunningham and Doug Williams were playing for," Moon said. "Even though we were playing for our teams and ourselves, we were also playing for our younger guys. We feel satisfied to see it come to fruition. We felt like we had something to do with that by the way we played."

Brad Johnson took over for an injured Moon midway through the 1996 season and showed potential, but when he was injured early in the 1998 season, Eagles castoff Randall Cunningham stepped in and responded with one of the most memorable seasons ever. Cunningham led the Vikings to a brilliant 15–1 record and threw 34 touchdown passes with only 10 interceptions. During the majority of his career in Philadelphia, Cunningham often made spectacular plays but was not always as

Randall Cunningham was brilliant during the Vikings' 15–1 season in 1998.

consistent as Eagles fans wanted him to be. During the 1998 season, Cunningham exceeded the expectations that were placed on him early in his career and the Vikings were the beneficiaries.

The following season, another veteran resurrected himself in Minnesota. Strong-armed Jeff George had worn out his welcome every place he had been in his career prior to arriving in Minnesota because of his petulant attitude and excuse making. But when he stepped into the Vikings offense midway through the season, he was all business and threw 23 touchdown passes while averaging a remarkable 8.56 yards per pass.

George was hopeful of holding down the quarterback spot after that, but Dennis Green had other plans. He had drafted the remarkable Daunte Culpepper from Central Florida in 1999 and after a year of watching how it got done in the NFL, Green wanted his mountain of a quarterback in the lineup. As a result, George was given his release.

As George tried to mount another comeback in 2006, he would have been more than willing to take any job offered. However, he truly wanted to return to Minnesota.

"My heart is still in Minnesota," George said. "I know that Brad Johnson is the quarterback there and I understand that and support him. But if he gets dinged up, I think I could help."

Nobody else associated with the Vikings shared that opinion.

At 6'4" and 265 pounds, Culpepper was built more like a defensive lineman or a big linebacker than a quarterback. Culpepper was a beast for defensive linemen to sack because of his size and strength.

Running back Robert Smith saw Culpepper at his first off-season workout after getting drafted and couldn't believe what he was looking at when the big man came into an offensive team meeting. Smith looked at Culpepper and thought he was a defensive lineman because of his size. When he realized who Culpepper was and that he was a quarterback, Smith realized that he was not looking at any ordinary rookie. "I thought he was in the wrong meeting," Smith said. "He looked like no quarterback I had ever seen."

Culpepper could run like a deer when he reached top speed, but it was his arm strength that had gotten him into the NFL.

"He throws the best deep ball of anyone in the NFL since John Elway," said Green. "He gets it there and it's very catchable."

The 2000 season was remarkable for Culpepper. In his first year as a starter, he threw 33 touchdown passes and ran for seven more. As fantasy players around the country hailed the arrival of their messiah, Green thought he had a quarterback that would lead the team to the Super Bowl.

But while Culpepper's ascension to stardom was quick, he could not maintain consistency. The 2001 season was a disaster as the Vikings fell to 5–11 and Culpepper threw just 14 touchdowns and had 13 interceptions. It didn't get much better in 2002 when the Vikings were 6–10 and Culpepper threw 23 interceptions.

The following year, the Vikings suffered heartbreak on the final play of the season. The only thing they needed to do was beat a lowly Arizona Cardinals team that came into the season finale with a 3–12 record. The Cardinals were particularly weak at defending the pass and it seemed as though the combination of Culpepper and Randy Moss would rip them apart. The Vikings

TRIVIA

Who became the first Vikings player to be inducted into the Pro Football Hall of Fame?

Find the answers on pages 193–194.

had a solid start, but they wilted in the desert and suffered an ignominious 18–17 defeat when Josh McCown threw a touchdown pass to Nathan Poole on the final play of the game. The humiliation and embarrassment were palpable and Vikings fans were spewing bile because the hated Packers had stolen the division title since they had pounded Denver 31–3 at home in their season finale.

Culpepper had bounced back in 2003 with a solid statistical year, but the painful finish ate at him throughout the off-season. He responded with a remarkable year in 2004, throwing 39 touchdown passes and completing 69.2 percent of his throws. He finished the year with an eye-catching 110.4 passer rating—the best ever by a Vikings quarterback.

It seemed as though Culpepper had finally found the balance he was searching for during the regular season, but after beating the Packers in Green Bay in the wild-card game, Culpepper could do very little in the 27–14 divisional playoff loss at Philadelphia.

In 2005 the roller coaster took a ride straight down. Culpepper was simply awful at the start of the season and the Vikings stumbled out of the gate. Culpepper had a tentative air about him and had just six touchdown passes to go along with 12 interceptions before he suffered an awful knee injury that ended his season.

Before the injury, the Vikings had seen enough. The thought of continued up-and-down performances from their quarterback was more than they could abide. He was traded to the Miami Dolphins for a second-round pick.

The Vikings went back to Johnson after Culpepper's injury and he also started in 2006. The aging Johnson struggled after a decent start and it's clear that the Vikings want to get better at the position.

History shows that they will do just that—and in memorable fashion.

DADDY DEAREST

GRANT'S LEGACY OF LEADERSHIP: BUD LEADS THE VIKINGS TO GREATNESS

Most people remember him standing on the sidelines at Metropolitan Stadium, wearing a stoic expression as the leader of a team that got close to football's version of nirvana but could never quite get the Super Bowl performance thing down.

Bud Grant and Marv Levy may share the disappointment of having lost four Super Bowls without ever knowing how winning one feels, but don't feel sorry for either man. Both have lived complete lives that include major interests outside the bastion of football.

Our focus is on Grant, a man so secure in himself and his abilities that he didn't care how his peers went about their business and he didn't model himself after anyone. Grant was always interested in doing as thorough a job as possible to get his team prepared and ready to play every season and every game within that season. He did not do that by getting to the office at 4:00 AM and then spending 18 hours of angst doing his job.

That was not Grant's way. He would prepare as much as he could in order to get his team ready—but not a minute more or a minute less. He didn't care if other coaches were spending more time on X's and O's and game plans and red zone charts. He was true to his conscience and he simply got the job done for the Vikings from 1967 through 1983 and then again in 1985.

Grant had a life outside football. A wife and six children told the world that icy and granite-like stares were not the full story. A love of outdoors and nature was just as important to him as doing his job well.

But don't take that as Grant doing anything but his best in leading the Vikings. He demanded discipline and self-respect from his players and got it without screaming and yelling. He was a natural leader on the sidelines who could communicate his disapproval with one look. One icy, blue-eyed stare from Grant was worth more on the sidelines than 1,000 words from Jon "Chucky" Gruden.

Grant has done much more with his life than simply become one of the most respected and successful coaches in NFL history. He was elected to the Pro Football Hall of Fame in 1994, leading a class that included Tony Dorsett, Jimmy Johnson (the 49ers defensive back, not the Cowboys coach), Leroy Kelly, Jackie Smith, and Randy White.

Grant's diversity of interests and ability to break free of the onerous demands of the profession made him something of a maverick. But Grant never left anything to chance on the football field. He was secure enough to know what he was doing and he did not vary from his game plan just because other coaches were doing it a different way.

GRANT TAKES THE REINS

Vikings owner Max Winter hired Bud Grant prior to the 1967 season as the Vikings head coach. Grant was a legend in the state before the Vikings came into existence. He was a tremendous two-sport athlete who had excelled at the University of Minnesota and had played professional basketball for the Minneapolis Lakers and had been a wide receiver for the Eagles in the NFL. Winter wanted Grant to become the coach in 1961, but Grant decided to honor his coaching commitment to the Winnipeg Blue Bombers of the Canadian Football League.

Norm Van Brocklin had coached the expansion team through its first six seasons and had proved to be a loud, opinionated, and emotional leader who tended to bully his players. Van Brocklin simply ran out of steam in Minnesota. After a season as a television commentator, Van Brocklin became the head coach of the Falcons during the 1968 season.

The Vikings were more than happy to see him go. Nobody was happier to see him leave than Fran Tarkenton, who had battled with Van Brocklin through each of those six seasons. Tarkenton anticipated a new beginning and a breath of fresh air around the Vikings.

However, Tarkenton didn't realize how fresh a start he was going to get. The Vikings traded him to the New York Giants for four draft picks a month after Van Brocklin's departure. Those draft choices were used to select offensive tackle Ron Yary, guard Ed White, running back Clint Jones, and wide receiver Bob Grim—all key members of Grant's team.

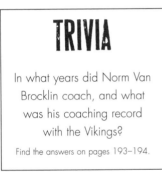

TRIVIA

In what years did Norm Van Brocklin coach, and what was his coaching record with the Vikings?

Find the answers on pages 193–194.

Grant and Jim Finks assembled a talented roster, but the coach knew the game was about more than athletic ability and physical skill. Grant wanted a team that had the stamp of toughness in its core and discipline as its trademark.

Playing outdoors at Metropolitan Stadium gave the Vikings a special advantage. Instead of providing heaters on the sidelines during cold weather, Grant preferred to have his team play in the cold weather. "We're prepared to have heaters if it gets cold enough," Grant said. "When there's a health hazard, like the Green Bay–Dallas [Ice Bowl] in 1967, we would use heaters.

"But some people can be cold at 68 degrees. I don't want players to look forward to being warm. Their attention should be on the field, not worrying where the heater is."

Grant wanted players who came from cold weather environments who could function in less-than-stellar conditions. Grant himself preferred playing outside in the elements as opposed to domes.

"There's no wind," Grant explained. "There's no rain. There's no snow. The temperature is constant. All of that takes away a lot of the coaching strategy of the game."

Grant also was one of the first head coaches to leave the specifics of game planning up to his assistants. His closest assistants were the ones who were getting in the trenches with his players and showing them the right way to play when they observed mistakes.

"I'm not a teacher," Grant said. "The assistant coaches are the technicians. I would go over the film a couple of times. They study it countless times. They present the actual game plan. Your staff can't be too strong. Then the head coach becomes the chairman of the board. I'm the guy they looked to for direction but the teaching comes from them."

Grant eventually came to that philosophy. But when he started his coaching career with Winnipeg in the Canadian Football League, he did it all.

"When I started coaching, I did everything," Grant explained in an interview with *American Football Monthly*. "With my first job as a head coach in Winnipeg [Blue Bombers], I did it all from the kicking game to the offense and the defenses. One of the reasons I was involved in all of it was because as a player I played every position on a football field with the exception of an interior lineman. As a pro player, I played tight end, wide receiver, linebacker, defensive end, safety, and cornerback. In high school, I was a running back and was able to call the plays. I had some experience at every position on a football team with the exception of the interior line.

"As I went along in my career, we acquired more and more assistant coaches, and then you turn over more of that to them, but with my background, I always had an understanding of what they were doing."

Grant was very well liked by the players. He was not overly demanding during training camp and he also knew how to treat people. "I don't like training camp," Grant explained. "It's the most unnatural thing in the world. When I came here, I had six kids and a wife at home and every summer I had to live in a dormitory for six weeks with a bunch of guys.

Bud Grant may have seemed expressionless on the sideline, but his players were always inspired and motivated by him. He treated his players well, but nobody dared to take advantage of him.

"We told our players to come to camp in shape and ready to work hard. If they did that, we kept camp to a minimum."

Grant's greatest ability as a head coach may have been his ability to get a quick read on his players' various personalities and then treat them accordingly. "Some you have to coax and kiss, others you have to drive," he said. "You must never belittle a man in front of his teammates. You get him aside, compliment him first, and then let him know what he is doing wrong."

Grant had an immediate impact on the team in his first year. The Vikings finished with a 3–8–3 record—nearly the same as the 4–9–1 record the year before. However, four of the Vikings' eight losses were by less than a touchdown. The team was much more alert and competitive. The Vikings were focused and had a new energy. Much of that had to do with quarterback Joe Kapp, an import from the Canadian Football League. Kapp struggled with accuracy in his first year in the NFL. He completed just 47.7 percent of his passes and he had an 8–17 touchdown-to-interception ratio.

Many coaches would have thrown up their hands and gone after a new quarterback, but Kapp had intangible characteristics that didn't come along very often. He was among the toughest quarterbacks to ever play in the NFL and there was a fire and magnetism to his personality that his teammates naturally followed.

TRIVIA

Which Vikings player once held the NFL record for most catches in a season, and what was that record?

Find the answers on pages 193–194.

By the following season, the Vikings were a playoff team with an 8–6 record. They lost to the Colts in the divisional playoffs, dropping a 24–14 decision in Baltimore. However, it was the beginning of one of the most dominant runs in league history. They would make the playoffs 10 times in 11 years, going to the Super Bowl in four of those years.

Grant attributed much of the team's success to a very basic factor—the high skill level of the players.

"You have to be able to assess talent," Grant said. "I don't think while I was here we ever let a player go who ever showed up on another team and played better than he played here."

Grant never had much use for the measurable qualities that are the staples of the modern draft, like how many times a player could bench press 225 pounds. "We never timed our players," Grant said. "I found out, for example, we could time a player and he would run a certain time, but if we ran him against another player he would run a better time. Well, that only told me that player, when faced with competition, ran a little bit faster or did something a little bit better. So times and weights and speed and all those things weren't as important. The most important thing was getting the job done.

"A good example was somebody like Paul Krause [Hall of Fame safety who played for the Vikings from 1968–1979]. If you tried to time Paul Krause, you would not even have him back the next day, but Paul Krause owns the interception record with 81 in his career.

"So we never timed the players. We were not interested in how fast they ran; it was just how well they did the job. You can measure them in all different ways: weights, heights, speeds, jump, go through all kinds of tests, everything you want. The one thing you don't measure is their heart and you can't put that down on paper. But you can create situations in practices and make observations of heart. He has to have great desire to be as good as he can be and that stems from what is inside of him."

The differences between Grant's reliance on his instincts for evaluating talent and the second-guessing that comes with the measurable qualities of today's scouting system is cavernous. But newer is not always better, especially in the case of a coach who had a dominant run while leading the Vikings to national prominence.

THE RETURN OF TARKENTON

The loss to the Chiefs in Super Bowl IV was one of Grant's major disappointments on the field, and the defeat had ramifications in the off-season. Kapp felt he needed to be compensated for his solid performance and outstanding leadership and held out in a contract dispute. Both sides hardened their positions and Kapp was traded to the Boston Patriots. The next two seasons resulted in playoff appearances, but no playoff wins, under quarterback Gary Cuozzo.

Finks and Grant realized they needed to get Tarkenton back from the New York Giants. Minnesota traded Bob Grim (who was obtained via one of the picks acquired in the original trade of Tarkenton to the Giants in 1967), Norm Snead, Vince Clements, a first round pick in 1972, and a third round pick in 1973 for Tarkenton.

After re-acquiring Tarkenton in 1972, Minnesota finished with a disappointing 7–7 season. Without the draft picks they lost, it would only be a momentary pause before they began a very

A COMMONSENSE APPROACH

The hiring process for NFL head coaches is a strange one. Teams can go for the "hot, young assistant" on the rise, the "disciplinarian" for a team that has too many loose cannons, the "player's coach" for a team that was beaten down by its previous coach. A team that struggled to put points on the board might look for an "offensive innovator." A team that gave up too many points needs a "defensive guru."

It seems that football coaches are specialists, concentrating on one side of the ball and letting their coordinator take care of the other side.

That specialization leads to a single-minded philosophy that makes it easy to label a coach as offensive-minded, old-school, or player-friendly. The point is that both the media and management love to stick a label on the coach that is hired to turn a team around.

The truth is that specializing in any one area won't turn a team into a winner and being married to any one particular philosophy won't work either.

Nobody understood this concept better than Grant. He tailored his philosophy to meet the talents of his players.

In the first part of his coaching tenure in the late 1960s, the Vikings had a couple of bulls in the backfield. Bill Brown and Dave Osborn were both power running backs and Grant tailored the offense around them.

When the Vikings reacquired Fran Tarkenton and drafted the elusive running back Chuck Foreman—one of the most underrated and versatile players in the game's history—Grant went to more of a short passing game.

When the Vikings added future TV celebrity Ahmad Rashad (an excellent receiver) and speedy wideout Sammy White, the Vikings became a big-play passing team.

Three different looks that made sense to employ. Grant was easily able to adapt his game plan because of the talent. He did not commit to just one style of play and the Vikings were able to ride his decisions all the way to the Super Bowl.

"I think the biggest mistake any coach can make is to hang on to the same playbook for 30 years and try to fit each and every player in some predetermined role," Grant said. "Some guys do certain things better than others, so why not use that to your advantage. It would have been silly of me to have Foreman run the same kind of plays as Osborn, just as the reverse is true as well."

The one thing that Grant really liked in his players was experience. Not only did Grant find veteran players reliable, he also trusted them with additional responsibilities. "On our teams the veterans did almost as much coaching as the coaches," Grant explained. "We had guys like linebacker Roy Winston and center Mick Tinglehoff who knew the defense and offense as well as anybody. They could pull a rookie aside and explain what was wrong and how to fix it."

Grant liked to let his players correct each other because there was none of the embarrassment that is often a byproduct of a coach's attempt to correct an on-field mistake. Grant never liked chewing out a player in public and always thought it did far more harm than good.

He thought that reading a player out publicly would hurt that player and also tear apart the team. "The other guys on the team see that and they have doubt in that player," Grant said. "How are they going to trust him if their coach doesn't trust him? That's why I never did it."

Grant was a man of few rules, but he coached as he lives and follows one rule every day. "Treat people the way you would like to be treated yourself."

That and his other common-sense approaches made his team consistent winners.

impressive run in the mid- to late 1970s. Chuck Foreman was drafted in the first round, out of Miami, in 1973, and a few other key offensive players, such as John Gilliam were added, all of which resulted in three more Super Bowl appearances—all losses.

Even though the Vikings developed a dominant defense that set NFL records, and the offense played an effective scheme that would later evolve into what would be termed the "West Coast offense," Minnesota's frustration was palpable.

Grant wanted to win those games as well, but he simply refused to dwell on defeats or over-celebrate victories. His visible expression always seemed to be the same whether the Vikings were winning or losing.

WHAT THEY SAID ABOUT BUD GRANT

"Bud Grant is a legend in the NFL. Bud's teams personified mental toughness and physical toughness. His teams started fast and hard, made the playoffs, and put together an outstanding record. The last impression is of Grant's team playing in the cold Met Stadium with strength, will, and determination."
—Dennis Green, former Vikings head coach

"Bud Grant has more leadership ability and more common sense than any person I have ever known or been around in my life. He was one of the very few great individuals that has ever been in this game."
—Fran Tarkenton, Hall of Fame quarterback

"Bud was very competitive. He knew how to pick people that were not only winners but had character. He knew how to pick people to win games and he surrounded himself with good players and coaches."
—Paul Krause, Hall of Fame free safety

"What made Bud great was his unique style of saying nothing, but communicating with a look that would make you play at 110 percent effort."
—Bob Lurtsema, former Vikings defensive lineman
and publisher of *Viking Update*

"Bud possessed great leadership and great intuition. If you were lost in the north woods in sub-zero weather with a group of men and you needed one individual to lead you to survival, Bud Grant would be your choice."
—Fred Zamberletti, Vikings trainer and team historian

"Bud Grant is one of the greatest coaches ever in the NFL. He is a victim of the Super Bowl losses we had. Bud Grant was the type of coach that told you what you needed to hear, not what you wanted to hear. He was fair with the guy who played on special teams and fair with the guy who was the superstar. Every job on the team was important, every player on the team was important. He treated every individual like a man."
—Chuck Foreman, former Vikings running back

"He's the supposed iceberg who sort of boils underneath. He enjoys a laugh better than anyone else I know. He is one of the finest people I've ever met. He treats everyone with dignity and respect. That's why players loved playing for him."

—John Michels, assistant coach, who worked for Grant throughout his career. Michels was with the Vikings from 1967 through 1993.

Grant was well aware of that tendency and had a reason that he rarely changed expressions while working the sidelines. "I've read a lot about what I do or don't do on the sidelines," Grant explained. "But to me football is a game of controlled emotion. If the head coach panics or loses his poise, then his team follows. When I see coaches running up and down the sidelines to yell at officials or players, then they lose sight of what is going on in the game."

With Bud Grant, what you see is not always what you get. He is a complex man who excelled at simplifying a very tough game.

GROWING THE PRODUCT

Jim Finks was one of the architects of the Vikings' glory years in the late 1960s and '70s.

Finks was one of the most versatile men associated with the NFL, playing seven years as a quarterback for the Steelers, serving 22 years as an administrator with the Vikings, Bears, and Saints, and finally emerging as a serious candidate for the commissioner's position after Pete Rozelle retired in 1989.

Finks helped turn the Vikings into winners, and he also had success with Chicago and New Orleans. Finks was hired in September 1964 as the team's second GM following the resignation of Bert Rose in June of that year. Finks came to the Vikings after a seven-year stint as general manager of the Canadian Football League's Calgary Stampeders.

Finks was not a poker player, but perhaps he should have been. Through shrewd use of the draft and a series of beneficial trades, the Finks-led Vikings soon began to take on a new look.

The team became more competitive and started to develop the kind of mental edge that goes with becoming a winner. Perhaps it was his history of living and working in Canada, but Finks looked at playing home games in the frozen tundra that was the Met in November and December as a major advantage for the Vikings.

"When we played teams like San Francisco, Los Angeles, or Dallas, it was clearly an advantage for us because we lived in the cold and we practiced in the cold," Finks said in 1987. "I really wanted us to develop the mentality of enjoying playing at home no matter what the weather was like."

Finks's building program began to pay dividends in 1968, when Minnesota won its first NFL Central division championship. That season marked the start of a dynasty that produced 11 divisional championship teams and four Super Bowl appearances in the next 13 years. In 1969, the Vikings won 12 of 14 games and claimed the NFL championship before losing to the Kansas City Chiefs 23–7 in Super Bowl IV.

The Vikings team that Finks helped assemble was powered by an incredible defense that was led by its athletic and nasty front four. The Purple Gang started with the acquisition of Jim Marshall from Cleveland in a 1961 trade. Finks had nothing to do with that trade, but in 1964, the new general manager added two potential stars to the line, end Carl Eller as a first-round pick in the NFL draft and tackle Gary Larsen in a trade. He completed the legendary unit in 1967 by picking Alan Page number one in the draft.

The group was physically talented and could dominate most opponents with their ability. But what allowed them to inherit the throne of the Los Angeles Rams' Fearsome Foursome was the teamwork and cooperation that developed through the unit.

"We knew what each other was going to do at all times," Marshall said. "We had great communication—and it wasn't only through the spoken word. I could look at Carl and he would know what I was doing and Alan could look at Gary and it would have the same impact."

In the modern NFL, that kind of connection would be impossible to develop. Finks put together a unit that played together from 1967 through 1975. Today, a coach would break down and cry tears of happiness at the thought of keeping any unit on his team together even half as long, let alone a group as important as the defensive line.

Finks was at his best in crisis situations. Late in 1966, Fran Tarkenton became embroiled in a feud with head coach Norm Van Brocklin. Finks solved the problem by trading the crowd-pleasing scrambler to the New York Giants for two first-round and two second-round draft picks, which he used to add more young, quality talent to the fold.

A few months later, Van Brocklin resigned and Finks immediately hired Bud Grant, a comparative unknown, as his new field leader. Grant had been a successful coach of the Winnipeg Blue Bombers of the CFL for 10 seasons.

"I saw Bud in good times and bad times in Winnipeg while I was in Calgary," Finks explained. "I know him as a man who knows how to win and how to retain his composure when he loses. And he isn't exactly obscure around here—he was an outstanding college athlete at Minnesota."

Grant also had another advantage that Finks was well aware of. He was not the explosive Van Brocklin. Grant had a presence that demanded respect, but he did not have to scream and yell to get it. He abhorred that attitude and he was

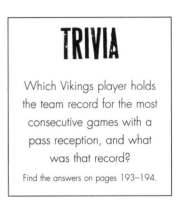

TRIVIA

Which Vikings player holds the team record for the most consecutive games with a pass reception, and what was that record?

Find the answers on pages 193–194.

clearly his own man and not a Vince Lombardi wannabe. He treated his players like men and if they chose not to act that way, he would have nothing to do with them. No ranting, no raving from Grant. He was a results-oriented coach who refused to lower himself by screaming and yelling needlessly.

Finks knew that type of personality was going to work wonders on a team that had grown weary of being berated and castigated by their head coach. The two combined for 10 division titles and three Super Bowl appearances (Grant added one more Super Bowl appearance after Finks left).

FINKS ON THE FIELD

Few remember that Jim Finks was one of the better quarterbacks in the league over a four-year span from 1952 through 1955. He led the league with 20 touchdown passes in 1952 and in passing yardage and completions in 1955. In his final season, the Steelers had a young quarterback named John Unitas, but head coach Walt "Keez" Kiesling did not feel it was necessary to give Unitas a chance to make the team since he had Finks and backup Ted Marchibroda on the roster.

Marchibroda would later go on to have a successful NFL head coaching career and developed a reputation as a great offensive innovator.

"Jim and I talked about it many times over the years and neither one of us remembered Johnny doing anything in camp," Marchibroda said. "He didn't do anything wrong and he didn't do anything memorable. You would think that a guy like Unitas would have made a big impression on his fellow quarterbacks, but he didn't because he never got a chance."

Kiesling was a conservative coach who had little use for the pass. He had little imagination or vision and cut Unitas without giving him an opportunity. Unitas, of course, went on to have a Hall of Fame career and is still considered the best quarterback in the history of the game according to many longtime observers.

In Tom Callahan's *Johnny U: The Life and Times of Johnny Unitas,* former NFL receiver Jimmy Orr explained that Kiesling was not always paying attention to his job. "Keez was still there when I was playing for the Steelers in the late 1950s," Orr said. "He was on the defensive staff and he was running the film projector. I had just gotten done with an offensive meeting and I walked past their room as the film ended. You heard the clickety-clack of the film ending and then a loud flap-flap-flap noise. Everybody in the room had fallen asleep, including Kiesling."

Finks had a solid playing career, throwing for 8,622 yards and 55 touchdowns in his career. But he was the first one to say that he was never in the same class as Unitas and only a sleepy coach like Kiesling would have failed to give him the opportunity he deserved.

Finks also brought in a new quarterback, Joe Kapp, from the CFL. Kapp, labeled "the Toughest Chicano" by *Sports Illustrated*, quickly became the Vikings' field leader. In the 1969 NFL championship season, he passed for a record seven touchdowns against Baltimore and was a major contributor to his team's success.

Kapp was not a pretty player by any stretch, but he might have been the toughest quarterback to play the game in the last half century. He brought an identity to the Vikings offense that forced opponents to take notice. Kapp initiated contact and absolutely refused to run out of bounds. He simply would not back down.

Unfortunately for Kapp, he took that same attitude into his contract negotiations with Finks. While he appreciated what Kapp had done for the team, he also recognized that his quarterback was not the second coming of Johnny Unitas or Bart Starr. Finks was a tough but fair negotiator who had heart and empathy. But a player who tried to threaten or intimidate him would pay a heavy price.

That was the case in 1970, when Kapp sat out some early games over a salary dispute. Finks sold Kapp to the Boston Patriots (they changed their affiliation to New England the following year) and turned over the quarterbacking chores to Gary Cuozzo, who had come to Minnesota in a 1968 trade with New Orleans. The Vikings kept right on winning with another 12–2 season and a third straight Central Division championship.

The Vikings won another Central Division title the following season, but they had been knocked out of the playoffs in the first round in both 1970 and '71.

As a result, Finks made another bold trade with the New York Giants. This time he brought Tarkenton back to the team five years after trading him. In 1973, they defeated the Dallas Cowboys for the NFC championship but dropped a 24–7 decision to the Miami Dolphins in Super Bowl VIII. It turned out to be the last game with the Vikings for Finks, who that season was named the NFL Executive of the Year.

A man of immense pride, Finks felt the Vikings were making a big mistake when team owners decided to build a new stadium in downtown Minneapolis. Finks's point of view was that the team belonged to the state of Minnesota and not just the city of Minneapolis. When owners did not listen to him, Finks decided to leave. He did not want to support ownership when he felt they were taking advantage of the team's loyal fans, so he resigned his position.

"They knew right where I stood," Finks said. "Our fans didn't want the stadium to go downtown."

Finks was not the sentimental type. His next job was with the Chicago Bears, and he led them back to respectability and ultimately glory as he ran the team for George Halas from 1974 through 1982.

TRIVIA

How many times have the Vikings had two of their kicks blocked in a game?

Find the answers on pages 193–194.

Many of the draft picks he made were instrumental in the Bears' 1985 Super Bowl run. They included Walter Payton, Dan Hampton, Otis Wilson, Matt Suhey, Keith Van Horne, Mike Singletary, and Jim McMahon. Nineteen of the 22 players who started in Chicago's 46–10 win over New England in Super Bowl XX were drafted during the Finks regime. That 1985 team went 15–1 in the regular season and shut out both the New York Giants and Los Angeles Rams in playoff games leading to the Super Bowl.

Finks did not stay with the team to see it win the championship. He had been angered by Halas's decision to hire Mike Ditka as head coach in 1982 without even asking him for an opinion.

Finks moved on to New Orleans, and he helped the Saints escape their history of losing by turning them into winners during his run from 1986 through 1993. His first move was to hire a new coach, Jim Mora, who had been very successful with the ill-fated USFL.

Success came more quickly for Finks in New Orleans than it had in either Minnesota or Chicago. In just his second season, the Saints won 12 of 15 games for their first winning season ever. Finks was named NFL Executive of the Year for a second time.

In the next five seasons, from 1988 to 1992, the Saints went over .500 four times and settled for an 8–8 year in 1990. In their last six seasons under Finks, the Saints won 62 and lost 33, a .653 winning pace.

Six players drafted by Finks—linebackers Sam Mills, Vaughan Johnson, and Pat Swilling, running backs Rueben Mayes and Dalton Hilliard, and special-teams player Bennie Thompson—made 16 Pro Bowl appearances during that period.

When Rozelle announced his intended retirement in 1989, Finks was the odds-on choice to replace him. A six-man search consisting of AFC president Lamar Hunt, NFC president Wellington Mara, Dan Rooney of Pittsburgh, Art Modell of Cleveland, Ralph Wilson of Buffalo, and Judge Robert Parins of Green Bay were charged with the responsibility of finding Rozelle's successor.

At an owners' meeting in May, the committee came up with 11 possible candidates. Two months later at a meeting in Chicago, Finks was their unanimous recommendation to become the new commissioner.

Rozelle called for additional nominees, but none were proposed. Rozelle called for the vote and 19 were needed to name Finks the new commissioner. He got 16 votes—but there were 11 abstentions.

There was a clear division among the owners and Rooney and Modell soon resigned from the committee. A new committee was formed with Hunt and Mara remaining as chairmen, but Minnesota's Mike Lynn, Ken Behring of Seattle, John Kent Cooke of Washington, and Raiders owner Al Davis now joined them. At a league meeting in Dallas in October, four more ballots were taken without any winner. However, Paul Tagliabue emerged as a clear challenger.

A few weeks later, the owners convened in Cleveland with yet another new committee. This group, which still included Lynn, made Tagliabue its unanimous choice. The "new guard" had gotten its way and defeated the "old guard." Finks was the casualty.

Publicly, the gracious Finks accepted the defeat: "I am proud that I was voted on by 19 of the 28 NFL teams. That makes me feel good."

However, he was very upset by the turn of events. He had wanted to become commissioner, believed he had the background for the job, and came within an eyelash of getting it before he fell short. As badly as he felt, Finks did not wallow. Tagliabue reached out to Finks and he accepted the key position of chairman of the league's competition committee.

During the next three seasons, Finks split his time between building the Saints and serving the league. His particular interest was in the game's rules. He urged sensible curbing of prolonged celebrations and made it clear he didn't like the "in the grasp" rules that protected passers when defenders first made contact.

Finks was serving a vital role for the Saints and the NFL when health issues forced him to resign in July 1993. He died less than a year later.

Finks's significant contributions to the Vikings, Bears, Saints, and the league itself earned him a posthumous Hall of Fame induction in 1995.

THE VIKINGS VISIT THE PETER PRINCIPLE: STECKEL'S DISASTROUS SEASON AS HEAD COACH

Les Steckel.

The name conjures up all kinds of nightmares for Vikings fans.

Steckel replaced Bud Grant as the Vikings coach prior to the 1984 season. Grant had been the head coach from 1967 through the 1983 season and decided to retire. Grant had been the team's stoic leader on the sidelines and the picture of consistency.

Grant was steady, proven, and rock solid. He might not have worn his emotion on his face as he strolled the sideline on game day, but his players knew exactly how he felt in the locker room and on the practice field.

Steckel was emotional, unsteady, and insecure. He wanted to come across as a Sergeant Rock type of disciplinarian, but there was little about his act that the Vikings were buying.

Steckel's militaristic attitude was part of his nature. He had enlisted in the Marines and served in Vietnam as an infantry officer.

There's a story that Steckel actually punched himself in the face in an effort to fire up his team. He recently revisited the anecdote. "What happened was one time I came into the locker room, and we were playing absolutely horrible," Steckel said. "I started grabbing people. I smacked my fist against my hand and all that kind of stuff, and I think I accidentally hit myself up by my cheekbone. I was trying my best to tell them there's one common denominator from the first day football was played, and it will be there until the last day, and that's physical toughness."

It wasn't his fault that he followed Grant, but that's how the job was offered to him. Steckel was a 38-year-old coach with five years of experience as a Vikings assistant. He had previously worked as an assistant football coach at Colorado from 1973 to 1976. He was an assistant at Navy in 1977, then an assistant with the San Francisco 49ers in 1978.

Steckel joined the Minnesota Vikings coaching staff as the receivers coach in 1979 and remained an assistant coach through the 1983 season. Grant believed the team would respond to his fiery leadership.

Instead, one of the most respected and consistent franchises in league history fractured into a million little pieces. By the time the 3–13 season was over, so was Steckel's head coaching career.

There were many aspects to the Vikings' season that should not be blamed on Steckel. The defense completely collapsed, giving up a monstrous 4.7 yards per rushing attempt and allowing 35 touchdown passes. The quarterback trio of Tommy Kramer, Wade Wilson, and Archie Manning was constantly under fire. None of the quarterbacks had a chance to get comfortable in the pocket and the trio of Vikings completed 52.7 percent of their passes. The offensive line was a mess, allowing 64 sacks.

The saddest sight during the season might have been the abuse that Wilson and Manning took in a game against the Bears in Chicago in late October. The Bears defense was just coming into its own under defensive coordinator Buddy Ryan's direction and the team's ferocious pass rush was on display on a blustery day in the Windy City.

The offensive line that included tackles Steve Riley and Tim Irwin along with guard Terry Tausch had no prayer at all against the likes of Dan Hampton, Steve McMichael, and Richard Dent.

Wilson and Manning were like sacrificial lambs as the Bears pass rush came at them in waves. By the time the game was over, the Vikings quarterbacks had been sacked 11 times. Minnesota had never suffered such carnage before or since. Manning, in the last year of an outstanding 15-year career, was no match for the youthful and mean-spirited Bears. He was tossed around like a rag doll being thrown against a wall by an overanxious five-year-old. He finished the game dazed and confused.

It got so bad that the normally vicious Bears felt sorry for Manning. After one brutal sack, linebacker Otis Wilson stood over Manning and begged him not to take any more punishment. "Don't get up, man," Wilson said. "Don't even get up. You need to stay down until they take you out of this game."

It was disaster for the Minnesota offense, but an affirmation for the Chicago defense that would go on to lead the team to the Super Bowl the following season.

"We had a great game that day," recalled Hampton. "It was the combination of us having a great day, they were having a bad day, and our system working. They did not know where we were coming from."

Steckel had no answers for problems presented by the Bears in that game or many others that year. Steckel's manner and decision making was open to question from the Week 1 kickoff against San Diego—a 42–13 defeat—to the season finale against the Packers—a 38–14 bludgeoning.

The Vikings' performance during the last six games of the season was proof that the team had nothing left to give Steckel. They lost their Week 14 game to the Redskins 31–17. All five of the other losses were by 21 points or more, including a 51–7 loss at San Francisco in Week 15 that many scouts believed was among the worst showings by an NFL team in the 1980s.

Steckel had many stops in his pro coaching career after he was fired by the Vikings at the end of the 1984 season. He went on to work as an assistant coach with the Patriots, Broncos, Oilers,

Titans, Bucs, and Bills before leaving the profession to become president of the Fellowship of Christian Athletes.

Steckel realizes that he probably wasn't ready for the job when it was offered to him. "If I had it to do over again I wouldn't have accepted the job," Steckel said. "As I look back on it, there are some people who are rather mature at age 37. I'm not sure I was. I didn't realize the scope and dimension of being a head coach. I was very sensitive to the fact that some great people, such as Jerry Burns and others, were not offered the job. I was sensitive to it but not very realistic about it. I made mistakes along the way. Not a few; many."

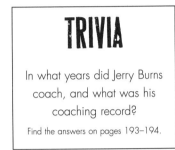

TRIVIA

In what years did Jerry Burns coach, and what was his coaching record?

Find the answers on pages 193–194.

Steckel never had another opportunity to become an NFL head coach, a fact that does not bother him. "It really doesn't. My wife and I say over and over how blessed we felt. People have strengths and weaknesses. I really believe my abilities lie in being an offensive coordinator. I loved the pressures of putting together the strategies and game plans for the week, and the game-day excitement of calling the plays. All the other stuff—contracts, off-the-field issues—didn't fire me up."

Steckel also pointed out that during the 1980s, many coaches did not get another chance once they got fired. "It's different now," Steckel said. "Look at Bill Belichick. He didn't have much success in Cleveland, but he got another chance in New England and look what he's done. I don't have any bitterness. I had my opportunity."

Steckel says he thinks he could get the job done as an NFL head coach if he had the opportunity, but it's not a burning desire.

Despite his unsuccessful run in Minnesota, the disastrous 2006 season under head coach Brad Childress had longtime fans recalling Steckel's regime with fondness.

Time heals all wounds.

WHEN THE FAT LADY SINGS

1975: HAIL MARY RUINS VIKINGS SEASON

After losing to the Steelers in Super Bowl IX, Bud Grant and the Vikings were determined to make the 1975 season a memorable one that would not end in failure. They made a preseason commitment to not get sidetracked by their 16–6 loss to Pittsburgh and instead get right back on track with Fran Tarkenton at quarterback, the versatile Chuck Foreman at running back, and a powerful defense that showed no signs of relenting.

Minnesota rolled through a 12–2 regular season, winning the NFC Central Division by five games over the 7–7 Detroit Lions. It appeared the Vikings were on a collision course with the equally powerful Los Angeles Rams, who were also 12–2 and dominant in their own right. The Vikings went into the postseason feeling like they would ultimately get back to the Super Bowl because they were awarded the top seed in the NFC and if they did play the Rams, it would be in the frozen hinterlands of Metropolitan Stadium.

But before the two heavyweights would battle for the NFC championship, there was a preliminary battle with the Dallas Cowboys that the Vikings would have to hurdle. The Cowboys were coming off a 10–4 regular season and had finished second to the Cardinals. They had played well in the second half of the season, but seemingly did not have the firepower on either side of the ball to stay with the Vikings for 60 minutes. They had lost stars Bob Lilly and Walt Garrison to retirement prior to the start of the year and 12 rookies made the team.

They did have a great quarterback in Roger Staubach, but the former Heisman Trophy winner from Navy was playing with bruised ribs that impacted his ability to throw the deep pass. "I know I can play," Staubach said before the game. "But I really feel it when I throw deep. That's going to be a very difficult throw to make against this team."

In addition to Staubach's physical issues, Dallas coach Tom Landry had legitimate concerns about containing Tarkenton. The Vikings quarterback had a brilliant season, completing 64.2 percent of his passes and putting 25 touchdown passes on the board. While he no longer was the scrambling runner he had been in his early years, Tarkenton played with a veteran's savvy and knew how to buy time with his quick feet while he waited for Foreman, John Gilliam, Ed Marinaro, and Stu Voigt to get open.

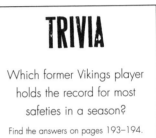

TRIVIA

Which former Vikings player holds the record for most safeties in a season?

Find the answers on pages 193–194.

"I don't know if we can contain Tarkenton," Landry said. "You really have to be patient against him. Our defense is young but we will have to grow up if we are going to be competitive against him."

The Vikings got on the scoreboard in the second quarter. After their drive stalled, Neil Clabo punted and Cliff Harris returned the ball to the Dallas 13-yard line. But Mick Tinglehoff had gone downfield too quickly and the Cowboys made the Vikings punt again. This time Clabo's punt bounced in front of Harris and apparently touched him before the Vikings' Fred McNeill recovered at the Dallas 4.

Three plays later, Foreman powered into the end zone from the 1.

Dallas was unable to do anything in the first half against a Vikings defense that had been stellar all season. It was still led by its veteran front four that included defensive ends Jim Marshall and Carl Eller along with defensive tackles Alan Page and Doug Sutherland, who had replaced run-stuffer supreme Gary Larsen.

But in the third quarter, Staubach led the Cowboys on a 72-yard touchdown drive that tied the game. On third-and-four from the Vikings' 4, the Minnesota coaching staff expected Staubach to throw the ball into the end zone. Instead, Landry fooled them by giving the ball to backup fullback Doug Dennison, who powered into the end zone from four yards out.

The Vikings were shocked by the play and later lost the lead when Toni Fritsch kicked a short field goal to give Dallas a 10–7 lead early in the fourth quarter.

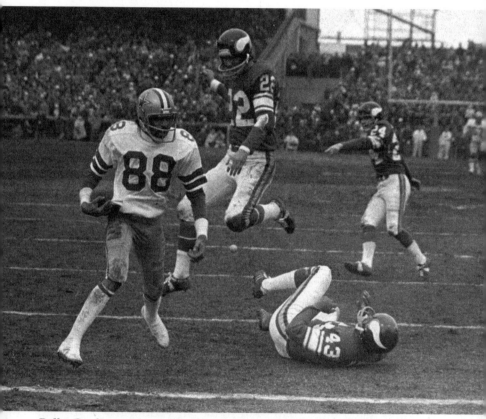

Dallas Cowboys wide receiver Drew Pearson trots into the end zone on December 28, 1975, after a game-winning 50-yard pass reception in the fourth quarter of the NFC playoff game in Minnesota.

The Dallas defense had stifled the Vikings throughout the game, but Tarkenton was not finished yet. The Vikings responded with a 70-yard drive that culminated with a one-yard plunge by running back Brent McClanahan.

Dallas was unable to move on its next possession and punted the ball back to the Vikings. With the two-minute warning approaching, the Vikings had a third-and-three. If they could convert, Grant's team would be able to run out the clock. Tarkenton kept the ball on a roll-out option, but Dallas safety Charlie Waters was blitzing and made the tackle.

The Vikings were forced to punt and the Cowboys took over at their own 15. With the weather getting colder by the minute and the game hanging in the balance, the Cowboys appeared to be out of chances. On a desperate fourth-and-16, Staubach was up against it. The Vikings pass rush was coming hard and the Minnesota fans had the Met rocking. One more stop and the Vikings would move on.

Staubach was not getting any help from the sidelines as Landry had him call his own plays inside the two-minute warning. Drew Pearson spoke up in the huddle and said he thought he could beat cornerback Nate Wright. Pearson ran a sideline pattern to the right side of the field and caught a pass just as he was going out of bounds. Referee Jerry Bergman ruled that the completion was good and the Cowboys had a first-and-10 at midfield.

TRIVIA

Who was the first player selected in the 1961 draft, the Vikings' inaugural year?

Find the answers on pages 193–194.

Staubach asked Pearson to run the same pattern only deeper, but Pearson said the play had left him gassed. The quarterback threw to Preston Pearson instead, but the pass was incomplete.

By then Pearson had caught his breath and was ready to go deep. There were 32 seconds left on the clock.

Staubach's ribs were hurting badly, but he knew he had to suck it up and make the throw. Pearson made a fake at the 15-yard mark before going downfield. Pearson turned it on and

A COWBOY'S PERSPECTIVE

On a dank, miserable afternoon in old Metropolitan Stadium, Roger Staubach threw up a 50-yard prayer. Down near the goal line, Drew Pearson answered it with an awkward one-handed catch and stepped into the end zone as stunned defender Nate Wright slipped on to the frozen field.

"I closed my eyes and said a Hail Mary," a wide-eyed Staubach said in the locker room after the game. "Then the prayer was answered."

The Hail Mary pass became an enduring source of joy for Cowboys fans, just as it became agony for Vikings fans. Staubach and Pearson still find people eager to talk about it wherever they go, and probably always will.

Of course, it would have been long since forgotten as just a long incompletion with 24 seconds left if Pearson hadn't trapped the ball on his right hip as he and Wright reached back for the underthrown pass. Wright stumbled to give Pearson a split-second chance for the catch.

"When the ball hit my hands, I thought I had dropped it," he said. "I said, 'Oh no, I blew it!' But I was bending over, and the ball just stuck between my elbow and my hip."

Pearson clutched the ball as he crossed the goal line, then held it high in triumph. The entire Cowboys team rushed on the field to celebrate while the Vikings blew their stacks. They howled that Pearson had pushed Wright down to get to the ball. The normally implacable Alan Page got so vociferous with his protest that officials assessed the Vikings a 15-yard penalty for unsportsmanlike conduct.

As the years went by and he was able to look at the play without emotion, Wright had no complaint about Pearson when he recalled his coverage on that play.

"I saw the ball in the air, and I really thought I could intercept it because I was in good position," Wright said. "Suddenly, my mind became confused. Next thing I knew I was on the ground, and I saw Drew catch the ball on his hip and run into the end zone. I was in shock."

Wright and Pearson agreed there was incidental jostling between them as they raced downfield but no intentional pushing when the ball came down.

> "I was looking for the ball out and away, and I felt I had one more gear to get past Nate, but then I saw the ball was under thrown," Pearson said. "Nate was running at an angle a little in front of me to cut me off if the ball went deep. But I came back with my arm in a swim move, reaching over Nate's shoulder for the ball. I was as surprised as anyone in that stadium that I caught that ball."
>
> But he did and one of the greatest Vikings seasons ever ended in the most painful fashion—outside of another Super Bowl defeat.

Staubach heaved the ball up. It was not a perfect Staubach throw. Instead, the Hail Mary pass wobbled and floated and came down short. Pearson had to wait for it with Wright quickly approaching, when suddenly Wright slipped and went down. Pearson made contact with the ball at the 5-yard line. It slithered around and he nearly dropped it, but regained control and stepped into the end zone.

The touchdown for the Cowboys ended the Vikings season but began a controversy. Why had Wright fallen down at the crucial moment? "He was pushed," said Grant.

"He seemed to slip," said Landry.

The controversy would never be forgotten in Minnesota, where Vikings players like guard Ed White thought their team was robbed.

It's a pain that still hurts in Minnesota to this very day.

A MIRACLE OF THEIR OWN

The Vikings remained a competitive team through the end of the Fran Tarkenton era in 1978. When that season ended, the Vikings had to remake the team and scramble to remain competitive. They struggled to do that in 1979 and finished in third place in the Black and Blue Division with a 7–9 record, but came back the next year to field a very competitive and hustling team.

Heading into Week 15 of the NFL season, the Vikings had an 8–6 record and were hosting a very strong Cleveland Browns team that would go on to win the AFC Central with an 11–5 record.

That Browns team, coached by Sam Rutigliano and quarterbacked by Brian Sipe, was known as the "Kardiac Kids" because of their ability to come back in the late stages of games and steal victories when all appeared lost. The Browns won eight games that season by seven points or less.

However, when they came to Metropolitan Stadium on December 14, 1980, they found out what it was like to be on the other end of a close decision.

Here's the unforgettable story of the Vikings' last-second win over the Browns that enabled them to clinch the NFC Central title.

The Vikings appeared to be in a hopeless situation. They trailed the Browns 23–22 with 12 seconds left on the clock and the ball at their own 20-yard line.

TRIVIA

When was the last time the Vikings had a shutout?

Find the answers on pages 193–194.

The Vikings had rallied after trailing 23–9 in the fourth quarter, but two missed Rich Danmeier extra points (one blocked) left them trailing. The team might not have been as strong as the great Vikings teams from the 1960s and '70s, but this group, which included quarterback Tommy Kramer, running back Ted Brown, and wide receivers Ahmad Rashad and Sammy White, played with heart and intelligence. Many of the fans in the stands were starting to head home, believing the team faced an impossible situation.

The Vikings broke the huddle, with Rashad, White, and wide receiver Terry LeCount lining to the right, in Hail Mary formation known to the Vikings as Squadron Right. Kramer dropped back, looked downfield to the right, but then fired over the middle at medium range. Tight end Joe Senser had come off the line of scrimmage and run a medium-range hook pattern. Senser made the catch and shoveled the ball off to the trailing running back Ted Brown on a hook-and-ladder play. Brown got free on the sideline and ran upfield to the Cleveland 47 before stepping out of bounds. Brown could have gotten perhaps 20 more yards, but he knew time was of the essence. He looked up at the clock and saw one second remaining.

Bud Grant did not vary from the formation he had on the previous play. Again he called Squadron Right, but this time Senser and Brown stayed in the backfield to block. Cleveland rushed its four defensive linemen, keeping the rest of their men deep downfield to prevent the game-winning touchdown.

Rashad, White, and LeCount raced down the right sideline—Rashad outside, White inside, LeCount in the middle. Kramer dropped back about 10 yards and then stepped up into the pocket and let the ball arc toward the end zone. The pass had unusual height on it and it came down at the five-yard line. It was met by the three Vikings receivers and six Cleveland defenders.

LeCount jumped as high as he could, but he found himself in a battle with Cleveland defensive back Thom Darden. The ball was actually tipped by Darden, but Ahmad Rashad, who was right behind the scrum and barely inside the sideline, reached out with his right hand and pulled the ball in. He backed up and made his way into the end zone for the game-winning touchdown.

Metropolitan Stadium erupted, roaring as they saw Rashad hold the ball up and then get mobbed by his fellow receivers. The old Met was shaking as the entire Vikings team ran down the sideline to mob Rashad in the corner of the end zone.

It was sudden victory for the Vikings and it gave Grant & Co. the NFC Central title. While they would lose a 31–16 decision to Philadelphia in the NFC divisional playoffs, the 1980 Vikings had made their mark with a never-to-be-forgotten storybook finish.

ON THE CUSP OF GREATNESS

1969: SEASON OF PROMISE

The Vikings took major strides in 1968 and then came on with a full gallop in 1969.

They were a full-fledged NFL juggernaut and Bud Grant had put together a simply superb outfit. Talk about toughness—the Vikings exuded it from every position, including quarterback.

Joe Kapp did not have the pedigree to compare with the game's top quarterbacks like Johnny Unitas, Bart Starr, or John Brodie, and many scouts said he wasn't even as talented as Roman Gabriel, Norm Snead, or Charley Johnson, but he had an intangible quality that got his teammates' attention.

"There was just something about Joe when he called a play," said running back Dave Osborn. "We believed in him. He had a fire, an inner confidence, and a desire that worked perfectly that season. Did he throw a pretty ball? Of course not. It would wobble and it wouldn't spiral but it would get there. He attacked people from the quarterback position and that's something that wasn't seen. It gave us a real charge to have him at quarterback."

With Osborn and Bill Brown running the ball, the Vikings put together a complete team with Gene Washington, John Henderson, and John Beasley catching it. Osborn was not a breakaway back, but he was very effective because he could slip tackles when he went to the outside and was effective running it between the tackles.

Brown was the definition of a football player from an era closer to the time of dinosaurs than today's football players. "Old football face" was a snarling pit bull of a fullback. Brown wrote the book on how to block from the fullback position while also maintaining his role as an effective insider runner. With his crew cut and aggressiveness, "Boom-Boom" personified Grant's desire to pound opponents and punish them as well as beat them on the scoreboard.

The key to the offense was an underrated offensive line that didn't get the notoriety of the Packers from previous years or the dominant Baltimore Colts, but the group included Grady Alderman at left tackle, Jim Vellone at left guard, Mick Tinglehoff at center, Milt Sunde at right guard, and Ron Yary at right tackle. Yary, the first offensive lineman ever selected with the number one pick of the draft back in 1968, would become one of the greatest linemen the game has ever seen.

Tinglehoff was one of the most underrated players in the game's history. He played in 240 consecutive games between 1962 and 1978—never missing even one game. Compared to the huge men who man the offensive line today, Tinglehoff was tiny. He checked in at 6'2" and 237 pounds. He was an incredibly consistent player who took over as the starting center during the second game of his first preseason and didn't give up the spot until he retired.

"He knew everything there was about the game," Kapp said. "He knew more about blocking than anybody I've ever seen but it was also his knowledge of whom he was going up against. He knew everybody's habits and tendencies. He was just a rock."

Amazingly, Tinglehoff was an undrafted free agent. Despite a fine career at Nebraska, no NFL team saw fit to select him even though the draft went 20 rounds. He simply responded to Minnesota's free-agent invitation and played like the best center in the game for the majority of his 17-year career.

The Vikings offense was clearly an effective unit that had the talent and toughness to win the battle most weeks. It was not an overwhelming unit by any stretch. The defense, however, was something to behold.

The Vikings' front four of Carl Eller, Alan Page, Gary Larsen, and Jim Marshall were a nightmare for quarterbacks throughout the NFL. The Purple People Eaters made a habit of destroying opposing offensive lines. Eller and Page are in the Pro Football Hall of Fame and Marshall probably should be. Larsen was the stay-at-home tackle who cleaned up all the running plays while the other three went after the quarterbacks.

Page was perhaps the most dominant defensive tackle to ever play the game. He recorded 108 sacks during his Vikings career and did it with a combination of speed and moves that have rarely been seen. In the late 1960s, most defensive tackles were big men who took up space in the middle of the line. They were expected to move about one body length to either side in order to make a play on the running back, and that was about it.

TRIVIA

Three of the Vikings' seven coaches won their first meetings with Green Bay. Who were they?

Find the answers on pages 193–194.

But with defensive tackles like Page and the Los Angeles Rams' Merlin Olsen, a new dimension was born. They could rush the passer from the middle of the line and collapse the pocket.

That's a familiar concept to NFL fans today, but in the 1960s pressure almost always came from the defensive ends on the outside. The pressure that came up the middle usually came on the blitz from the middle linebacker or safety. Tackles were expected to hold their position and little else—until Page started to shred offensive lines with speed and quickness.

"I found that if I attacked quickly and got my hands on the offensive lineman first I could make a move and usually get into the backfield," Page said. "My speed gave me an advantage when it came to getting to the quarterback, the running back, or whomever had the ball. If I could get off the first move at the instant the ball was snapped, I knew I could win the battle."

Eller was the ferocious type who played with a nasty scowl that intimidated more than a few opponents. Like Page, he had plenty of speed and quickness that allowed him to win the battle with opposing right tackles, but he also enjoyed punishing opponents. One of his frequent opponents was Packers right tackle Forrest Gregg, who is in the Hall of Fame himself. Gregg's career ended following the 1971 season and he knew the end was near because he could not handle Eller's speed and ability to string moves together.

If the Vikings were overwhelming on the defensive line, they were brainy at the linebacker spot. Nobody seemed to understand their schemes any more than Wally Hilgenberg, who was an unimposing 6'3" and 229 pounds, but would regularly diagnose plays and put himself in the right position.

The secondary was led by free safety Paul Krause and aggressive cornerback Bobby Bryant. Krause was the leader of the unit and became the NFL's all-time leader in interceptions with 81. He had the instincts for the position that so few safeties have today. Bryant led the Vikings with eight interceptions and fellow cornerback Earsell Mackbee was right behind with six picks.

The success of the defensive backs was thanks in large part to the havoc created by the defensive line. "We knew that if we could put pressure on the quarterback it was going to pay off with turnovers," Page said. "You get to the quarterback in the beginning of the game and he doesn't want to keep getting hit. These guys were not stupid and didn't want the pain. They see Carl coming or feel Jim [Marshall] going around the corner or see me coming up the middle and the ball was going to be put up a little early. That's what we were trying to do as a unit."

Nobody did it better in 1969—at least in the NFL. Minnesota lost its first game of the season to the New York Giants and lost their regular-season finale to an awful Atlanta Falcons team. But they won all 12 games in the middle and beat the Rams in the Western Conference championship and dominated the Browns in the last NFL championship game.

The Super Bowl might have been a different story, but the Vikings had an identity and a position in the NFL that they would hold for a decade.

THE CUNNINGHAM FACTOR

Cunningham started the '98 season as a backup to Johnson, but was quickly thrust into the limelight when a broken leg sidelined the starter in the second game of the season against the Rams. He ended the year as the league's MVP.

"Here's the amazing thing," Billick said. "You had all the stereotypes—he can't work within a structured offense, can't read coverages, is selfish. All the things we heard. And here we sit. He's probably one of the most unselfish players I've ever been around."

Cunningham, who lived on the run during 11 seasons in Philadelphia, stayed in the pocket with the Vikings.

Cunningham finished the regular season completing 60.9 percent of his 425 passes with 34 touchdowns, 10 interceptions, and a passer rating of 106.0—the best in the NFL that season and more than 14 points higher than his previous high of 91.6 set in '90, when he was awarded several player-of-the-year honors.

"I'm very patient now," Cunningham said at the conclusion of the regular season. "I think that's one of the things about my game on the field that has changed. I'm patient. I can drop back and not worry about who's picked up and who's not picked up. Look down the field. Focus and fire. In Philly, I used to drop back, and I had fear."

Under Billick's direction, Cunningham was asked to drop back and go through a progression of reads. With an offensive line that included three Pro Bowlers, Cunningham had time to do just that—and the results were incredible.

Cunningham was the first to admit that his surrounding cast of Carter, Moss, Smith, and Reed had much to do with his success. "It was like a dream team," Cunningham said. "There was so much talent, but it was more than that. We really meshed well together."

Cunningham was the triggerman. He had always thrown a beautiful deep pass and he added an intermediate phase that kept opponents off balance.

"There were others who throw more touchdown passes," Billick said. "But, within the confines of the team, to say what quarterback had the best season in the history of the league? His quarterback rating, success of our team, success of the offense—a case could be made for Cunningham."

DIAMOND WITH A FLAW: THE CURSED SEASON OF 1998

When the Vikings look back at the brilliance that was the 1998 season, it ends up as a bittersweet memory. Minnesota won 15 of its 16 regular-season games and had the most prolific offense in the history of the game, scoring a league-record 556 points during the season.

With Dennis Green running the show and a brilliant game plan provided by offensive coordinator Brian Billick, Minnesota left the rest of the NFL in its wake during the regular season. However, the expected cruise through the NFC playoffs to a Super Bowl date with the Denver Broncos in Miami was short circuited.

That didn't happen because the Vikings dropped the NFC championship game at home to Atlanta. The Falcons could not match Minnesota in talent, but Dan Reeves had a confident, perhaps even arrogant team that believed it could do the impossible by felling the Vikings in their own backyard.

There is no doubt that the season ended with a major hangover for Minnesota, but the rest of the year was brilliant. The Vikings had high expectations at the start of the year, thanks in large part to what appeared to be an explosive offense. Randall Cunningham backed up Brad Johnson at quarterback, giving them security at the most important position. Robert Smith was one of the fastest and most explosive running backs in the game. Leroy Hoard showed his gifts on short-yardage plays. Cris Carter was widely recognized as the number two wide receiver in the league behind San Francisco's Jerry Rice, but perhaps made up for that difference with the leadership he brought to the team.

But what really threw the Vikings into overdrive was the presence of a spectacular rookie. Randy Moss came out of Marshall as the clear number one receiver in a class that included Kevin Dyson of Utah, Marcus Nash of Tennessee, Jacquez Green of Florida, and Joe Jurevicius of Penn State.

There was no comparison between Moss and the others in terms of talent, game-breaking ability, or potential. But the NFL was afraid of Moss—afraid of his background, which included a guilty plea to a battery charge as a result of his participation in a racially motivated fight and a 60-day jail sentence as a result of a marijuana charge. NFL teams thought long and hard about his positives and negatives before the draft. Even though most scouts recognized that Moss had the talent to be taken within the top five picks of the draft, he fell all the way to the Vikings with the number 21 selection.

Green welcomed him as if he was a football god. Nicknamed "the Freak" because of his monstrous athletic talent—speed, quickness, jumping ability, hand-eye coordination, combined with a 6'4", 210-pound frame—Moss was clearly the X factor for the Vikings. If he fit into Billick's big-play offense, the Vikings could be unstoppable. If he reverted to the undisciplined ways that had gotten him into trouble before the start of his college career, he could tear the team apart.

TRIVIA

When did the Vikings get their first win against Green Bay at Lambeau Field?

Find the answers on pages 193–194.

During the first part of his career in general and the first season in particular, Moss was spectacular. He caught 69 passes for 1,313 yards and an amazing 17 touchdowns. The Vikings became an impossible team to stop because they had too many devastating options. It was an embarrassing wealth of riches for Billick.

"Everything just meshed for us that season," Billick said. "We were able to go downfield and stretch the defense with two great receivers. Our running game was capable of breaking big plays. The offensive line was big, strong, and capable. The quarterback play was efficient when it needed to be and also capable of the big throws. It all worked. You couldn't have asked for more."

The record book bears this out. The Vikings became a relentless touchdown machine, putting more points on the board than Bill Walsh's great 49ers teams, Joe Gibbs's Redskins, or the prolific offense that Mike Martz had in St. Louis. They became the highest-scoring team in the history of the game with the ability to blitz opponents with two or three touchdowns in a matter of minutes.

The Vikings also got a major boost from special teams as veteran place-kicker Gary Anderson had the best season of his distinguished

23-year career and was one of two kickers in the league with 20 or more attempts to have a perfect regular season. Gary Anderson made all 35 of his attempts—including two from 50 yards or more.

While the Vikings were superior on the offensive side of the ball, they more than held their own on the defensive side. Linebacker Ed McDaniel was an honest player who gave his all on every play and led the team in tackles with 155. Emotional John Randle was the sack leader on the defensive line with 10.5 quarterback traps. Cornerback Jimmy Hitchcock was an average cover guy, but he led the team with seven interceptions.

Combine the offense, defense, and special teams with a driven coaching staff and the Vikings were nearly perfect. The only blemish was a 27–24 defeat at Tampa Bay in Week 8. The Vikings appeared to be in charge with a 24–17 lead in the fourth quarter, but they wilted in the heat and humidity of central Florida and dropped their only game when Mike Alstott pounded the ball into the end zone with 5:48 remaining in the fourth quarter and the Vikings could not respond.

Randy Moss electrified Vikings fans during his spectacular 1998 rookie season.

That little defect did not stop the Vikings from joining the 1984 49ers and 1985 Bears from finishing the regular season with a league-record 15 wins. (The 2004 Steelers would eventually match that record as well.) But the season ended in defeat—a fact the franchise will never get over until the Vikings finally win football's holy grail.

The Key Moments

The Green Bay Packers had an excellent season in 1998. They had won the Super Bowl two years earlier, gotten back there in '97, and were the clear favorites to win the NFC Central again.

The Packers knew that the Vikings had talent and were going to be a force, especially when they rolled into Lambeau Field for a Week 5 Monday night game with a 4–0 record. But in their heart of hearts, they believed the Vikings would collapse under the pressure of the moment and that they had no answers for Brett Favre. The Packers also had another thing going for them: a little thing called a 25-game home winning streak that was the second longest in NFL history. To say that the Packers were confident when playing at home is like saying Bill Gates is not worried about where his next meal is coming from.

Were the Vikings intimidated? Not a bit. They walked into Lambeau like they owned it and punished the Packers.

Like a heavyweight fight, there was a feeling out process in the first quarter, with both teams wary about showing what they could do. Gary Anderson got the Vikes on the board with a 33-yard field goal and Ryan Longwell answered early in the second quarter with a 40-yarder of his own.

Cunningham thought that was enough and started to open things up. He hit Jake Reed with a 56-yard scoring pass that had the Packers defense wondering what happened. They got a momentary reprieve when Roell Preston returned the ensuing kickoff 101 yards for a touchdown. It was to be their last significant play in the game.

Within moments, Randy Moss was showing the Lambeau faithful that the balance of power was shifting in the division. He brought in a spectacular 52-yard touchdown pass from

Cunningham and the Vikings added another before halftime when Robert Smith caught a 24-yarder.

Two more Anderson field goals preceded a 44-yard touchdown hookup between Cunningham and Moss. The Vikings had stretched their lead to 37–10 with 10 minutes remaining. The Packers managed two cosmetic touchdowns in the final minutes, but their home winning streak had been devastated.

Green Bay would go on to a fine 11–5 season, which is normally good enough to contend for the division title. But all it got them in '98 was second place and a wild-card road game at San Francisco that would end in a painful defeat.

After dropping their game at Tampa Bay, the Vikings got back on track with home wins over the Saints, Bengals, and Packers. Then came another offensive explosion before another national audience. They went to Dallas on Thanksgiving Day and outscored the Cowboys 46–36. Moss once again had a little something to do with the output. He only caught three passes in the game, but all three were for spectacular touchdowns. He scored in the game's first two minutes on a 51-yard pass from Cunningham and added two 56-yarders—one in the first quarter and one in the third.

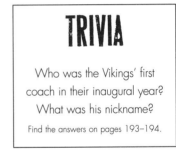

TRIVIA

Who was the Vikings' first coach in their inaugural year? What was his nickname?

Find the answers on pages 193–194.

It wasn't just Moss wreaking havoc on the Cowboys. Dallas owner Jerry Jones could do little more than put his face in his hands as Cris Carter caught a 54-yard scoring pass and Leroy Hoard had a 50-yard run. Dallas would go on to win the NFC East title, but that game took away much of their swagger and confidence. They would not get out of the first round of the postseason.

Five touchdowns of 50 yards or longer did more than just thrill fantasy leaguers who had stocked their rosters with Vikings. It served notice on the rest of the league that the Vikings offense was capable of striking from anywhere, at any time.

They did it again the following week at home against a hapless Bears team, rolling to a 48–22 win. If that wasn't enough,

Running back Robert Smith helped fuel the Vikings' high-flying offense in 1998.

the Vikings embarrassed the Jacksonville Jaguars in Week 16 with a 50–10 runaway. Moss was once again involved, catching a 43-yard touchdown pass early in the third quarter to set the runaway in motion.

They closed the regular season with a 26–16 win in Tennessee against the Oilers—they would change their name to Titans the next year—and joined the 49ers (1984) and Bears (1985) as the only teams to win 15 games in a season. The 2004 Steelers would later tie that mark, but it was clear that Green's team had joined a very exclusive club.

Playoff Heartbreaker

As the postseason started, the Vikings were clear favorites to represent the NFC in the Super Bowl. The defending Super Bowl champion Broncos looked imposing with John Elway, Rod Smith, and Terrell Davis, and fans were looking forward to a Minnesota-Denver matchup because of the star power on both sides.

That game would have matched two of the game's premier offensive strategists in Billick and Denver's Mike Shanahan. It might have been the highest scoring Super Bowl in the game's history.

However, Dan Reeves and his Atlanta Falcons failed to get the memo.

"The Dirty Birds" had gone 14–2 with accurate-throwing Chris Chandler at quarterback and a thieving defense (44 take-aways) that featured the pass rushing of defensive end Chuck Smith. The nasty Smith—even his teammates stayed away from him—had an outside rush and a claw move that was frightening to most right tackles in the league.

Minnesota dispatched Arizona 41–21 in the divisional play-offs. The performance was rather ho-hum by Vikings standards because the Cardinals were not a very strong team—they finished 9–7 in the regular season and upset the Cowboys in the wild-card round—but there was no reason for alarm.

Green knew his team would have to step it up against the Falcons in the NFC championship. Atlanta had edged San Francisco 20–18 in their playoff meeting. The game appeared to take everything out of the winners and it earned them a trip to the mind-numbingly loud Metrodome.

Reeves played the disrespect card to the hilt in order to get his team ready. The Falcons were double-digit underdogs and it was just a matter of how much the Vikings would win by and when the game would be over. The Vikings wanted to have this game well in hand by halftime so they could start making their Super Bowl plans.

But the Falcons stood up to an early barrage and did not flinch. The Vikings built a 20–7 lead with 1:17 remaining in the first half, which was normally the type of situation that would allow them to put an opponent away.

That's when Coach Green and offensive coordinator Brian Billick got greedy, ordered three downfield passes, and watched in horror as Chuck Smith beat tackle Todd Steussie around the corner and forced Cunningham to fumble on the third down.

Atlanta recovered at the 14 and Chandler hit the wide-open Terance Mathis for a touchdown on the next play, giving the Falcons halftime hope.

"That was our style all year," Green said. "We had been one of the most successful teams in the league doing that. We were trying to put them away."

With 2:07 remaining in regulation and the Vikings ahead 27–20, the Vikings gave the Falcons more hope. Place-kicker Gary Anderson came on to cap a 10-play drive of 54 yards but missed barely wide left from 38 yards. It was his first miss of the season.

"His misfortune was our fortune," Falcons safety Eugene Robinson said.

The Vikings secondary, on the vulnerable side all season for a team with designs on best-ever recognition, blew a coverage and Ronnie Harris caught a 39-yard pass at the Minnesota 31. From there, strong safety Robert Griffith failed to handle a deflection in the end zone that would have been a game-saving interception and, on the next play, Chandler found Mathis against tight coverage for the tying touchdown.

TRIVIA

In what year was the Vikings' first overtime game?

Find the answers on pages 193–194.

The game went to overtime and Morten Andersen's 38-yard field goal with 3:07 left in the first extra session sent the Falcons to the Super Bowl and provided a profoundly disappointing end to the Vikings season.

Green tried to maintain his dignity after the game, but the pain and disappointment was palpable. "This was a solid season but not the great season that we really wanted," Green said through clenched teeth.

"We had been so good and so consistent throughout the season," Cunningham said. "It really hurt when we lost that game. We had everything going for us. A big lead, the crowd was roaring, but we just couldn't get the job done."

This had been a team that had bludgeoned and bullied its opponents. But the Falcons stood up to their 1-2 combination and had not flinched. That was enough to throw the Vikings off track and prevent them from meeting their goals—a sad way for a brilliant season to come to an end.

100

SOCIAL PROGRESS

DENNIS GREEN: MAN OF MANY FACES

He might not have brought the Vikings to the Super Bowl, but Dennis Green is clearly the second most successful coach the Vikings have had, behind Bud Grant.

During his 10-year run between 1992 and 2001, the Vikings made the playoffs eight times. The 49ers and Cowboys made it seven times each during that span.

Green was an enigma to Vikings fans. They loved him because he was able to win so consistently during the regular season, but they were disappointed because the team was such a flop in the postseason. The Vikings had a 4–8 postseason mark under Green, never winning more than one game in any postseason and dropping their first four before they discovered a way to sneak out of Giants Stadium with a 23–22 run following the 1997 season.

It's difficult to characterize Green's coaching regime. True, there were many regular-season accomplishments, including a brilliant 15–1 mark in 1998, but the team's failure to live up to its potential and its propensity for falling into so many postseason traps haunted Green's career in Minnesota.

Perhaps the most impressive aspect of Green's tenure was the fact that he was able to win consistently even though he constantly had to change his quarterbacks. Green made those eight appearances with seven signal-callers, an accomplishment unprecedented in NFL history. His ability to build a consistent

TRIVIA

What did Norm Van Brocklin call the players on his roster in 1961?

Find the answers on pages 193–194.

offense despite the many changes at the game's key position was solid testimony to his ability. It started with Rich Gannon and Sean Salisbury in 1992, aging Jim McMahon followed the next year, before Warren Moon took over in 1994. Moon shared the job with Brad Johnson in 1996—they missed the playoffs in 1995—and Johnson took over as the starter in 1997. Their brilliant '98 season came with the comeback of Randall Cunningham, who had retired a couple of years earlier and served as Johnson's backup in '97. Jeff George took over for the injured Cunningham in 1999 and commandeered an explosive down-the-field offense before giving the ball to a young phenom in Daunte Culpepper in 2000. Culpepper was a raw draft choice from Central Florida who brought size, athleticism, and a strong arm with him. Green helped make him a productive player quicker than most scouts thought possible.

Green also had a way of handling troubled players and getting the most out of them. The most significant examples were wide receivers Cris Carter and Randy Moss. The Vikings signed Carter in 1990 after he was unceremoniously cut from the Eagles by Buddy Ryan. Carter, troubled by alcohol and drug use, was clearly a talented player who was coming off a season in which he caught 45 passes for 605 yards and 11 touchdowns, but Ryan had no doubts about cutting him. His message to the receiver upon delivering the news to him was that he could no longer depend on him to perform.

Carter made a harsh personal assessment of himself as he came to grips with his dismissal from the Eagles. Instead of behaving like a petulant, spoiled athlete and blaming Ryan, he vowed to change his work habits, consistency, and off-the-field activities.

He got nothing but encouragement from Green after the Vikings signed him and made him their number one receiver. Minnesota was the right place for Carter and he signed with the team at the right time. His new attitude, along with Green's positive reinforcement, helped Carter to become the number two receiver in the league with 1,101 receptions—trailing only Jerry Rice.

Carter credited Green's attitude with helping him to turn things around. Unlike many football coaches, Green did not make a lot of petty demands on his players. Much like Bud Grant, he gave his players a chance to act professionally before he imposed consequences.

"Dennis treats his players like men," Carter said. "He treats them with respect. As a result, he gets respect back."

Moss was a brilliant talent as a star at Marshall during his college career. But there were many off-the-field concerns that made him drop like a stone in the 1998 NFL draft. Even though he was clearly talented enough to be a top three draft pick, teams were afraid to draft him and he fell to the Vikings with the 21st pick in the draft.

GREEN'S ACHIEVEMENTS WITH THE VIKINGS

- Most trips to the playoffs, 1992–2000: eight, all under Dennis Green, with seven different quarterbacks
- The only coach to reach the playoffs in each of the five seasons of 1996–2000
- The only team to qualify for the playoffs each of the four years, 1997–2000
- One of only four to coach team to win 15 games in a single season. Bill Walsh of the 49ers (1984), Mike Ditka of the Bears (1985), and Bill Cowher of the Steelers (2004) were the others
- Wins regardless of the playing surface, temperature, home or away. Coached winning records outside (33–24), in domes (59–28), on grass (23–20), on artificial turf (69–32), and in temperatures below 40 degrees (7–3)
- One of only eight men in NFL history to lead his team to the playoffs in each of his first three seasons (1992–94) as a head coach
- Highest winning percentage in Vikings history (1998, 15–1, .938)
- Best League record 1992–2000: 92 wins against 52 losses (.639)

GREEN'S SPECIALTY—DEVELOPING QUARTERBACKS

If Dennis Green can hang his hat on any one particular aspect of coaching during his time with the Vikings, it was his ability to bring quarterbacks along quickly and help them reach the top of their game.

Green inherited Rich Gannon as his starting quarterback in 1992 and the head coach recognized that he had a signal caller with mobility and accuracy working for him. Gannon split time with Sean Salisbury at quarterback and the Vikings finished 11–5 with a very productive offense that outscored their opponents by 125 points.

The rest of the NFL did not truly notice Green's talent as a head coach and as a guy who could get the most out of his quarterbacks until the following season. Forced to use an aging and limited Jim McMahon at the position, Green coaxed a 9–7 playoff season out of his team. McMahon found a way to complete 200 of 331 passes for 1,968 yards with nine touchdowns and eight interceptions and was able to get the job done with moxie and grit as his primary tools.

Warren Moon finished his Hall of Fame career with a 2½-year stint with the Vikings starting in 1994. While most of the football world thought Moon was finished, Green expressed his confidence that Moon was still a productive signal caller who could make every throw in the book. "Warren was a surefire Hall of Famer and we were lucky to get him," Green said. "He was everything we thought he would be and there's no doubt how much he helped this team."

Brad Johnson had proven little when he took over from Moon midway through the 1996 season, but Green liked his accurate arm and ability to wait until the last instant to find open receivers. After a mysterious neck injury, Green proved he was an absolute genius with his ability to handle the game's most vital position.

He brought Randall Cunningham out of retirement. After working full time in the tile business while residing in Las Vegas in 1996, Cunningham put on a Vikings uniform in 1997. Cunningham had been a magician during his career with the Eagles, but he had acquired a reputation as one of the game's premier prima donnas during his 11-year run in Philadelphia. He could make the most spectacular highlight-film plays—a 60-yard off-balance throw from the end zone to Fred Barnett that resulted in a 95-yard touchdown in 1990 at Buffalo remains an unbelievable achievement—but he bought into his own superstar status and was difficult for most teammates to stomach.

A year away from the game humbled Cunningham, who realized how much he was missing. He was grateful for the opportunity Green gave him, and when he led a comeback win over the Giants on the road in the wild-card playoff game, the Vikings coach knew he had his quarterback for the 1998 season.

Green knew Cunningham was one of the top quarterbacks in the league, but he could not have even dreamed of the way his team would roll to a 15–1 mark. Cunningham threw 34 touchdown passes and just 10 interceptions and made it to his fourth Pro Bowl.

Jeff George was nearly a football pariah when he was signed by the Vikings in 1999. His pouty demeanor and reputation for sulking nearly overwhelmed the magnificent arm he brought to the game. After stints in Indianapolis, Atlanta, and Oakland ended in disappointment, he enjoyed a brilliant 1999 season after taking over from the injured Cunningham. Suddenly, George was happy and productive. He completed 191 of 329 passes for 2,816 yards with 23 touchdowns and 12 interceptions. His ability to throw the deep ball opened things up for Robert Smith (1,015 yards) and Leroy Hoard (555 yards) in the running game.

Despite his fine season that included a 27–10 win over Dallas in the postseason, the Vikings did not re-sign George. They drafted the multitalented Daunte Culpepper in the first round in 1999 and deemed him ready for action in 2000. Green did a great job of harnessing Culpepper's natural ability and turning him into a force. Not only did Culpepper throw 33 touchdown passes, he also ran for seven touchdowns.

Culpepper's performance was the final installment in Green's production of "As the Quarterback Turns" during his memorable run in Minnesota.

Again, Green made him feel welcome and gave him an environment in which he could be productive. Instead of keeping Moss on a short leash, he explained the rules to his newest star and let him go on the field and do his thing. At the same time, Carter took an interest in Moss and tried to influence him.

It certainly worked that season as the Vikings set an NFL record for points scored with 556 in the '98 season. The Vikings were virtually unstoppable on the offensive side of the ball, terrorizing defenses with Carter and Moss at the wide receiver position, Randall Cunningham at quarterback, and Brian Billick calling plays under Green's leadership.

"We had the kind of balance needed to be a truly dangerous team," said running back Robert Smith, who led the team with 1,187 yards and a 4.8 yards per carry average. "They didn't know if we would throw it deep, throw it short, run it. And you know what, it probably wouldn't have mattered if they did because we executed so well. We had fun that season every time we went out there."

The Vikings did things that no other team has done before or since. In a four-game span against the Cowboys, Bears, Ravens, and Jaguars, they scored 182 points for an average of 45.5 points per game. The impressive production might have built a false sense of security when the Vikings went into the postseason.

The 1998 NFC championship loss to the Falcons was really the beginning of the end for Green in Minnesota. While the Vikings had playoff seasons in 1999 and 2000, they were not the same team they had been in 1998. They were simply not as powerful and not as dangerous. The feeling was largely unspoken, but nearly everyone around the team came to the same conclusion. If they couldn't win in '98 with their powerful offense and 15–1 record, when would Green ever lead them to a title?

That conclusion was driven home two years later when the Vikings finished 11–5 and went to the NFC championship against the New York Giants after beating New Orleans 34–16 in the divisional playoffs. The Vikings were underdogs as visitors to Giants Stadium, but a close game was expected. Instead, Green's team looked unprepared and uninspired in a 41–0 blowout loss.

The embarrassment was more than owner Red McCombs could handle. Green stayed on the job, but he was fired less than a year later.

Green announced his departure from the Minnesota Vikings at a news conference at the team's headquarters. "I will no longer be the head football coach and vice president of football operations for the Minnesota Vikings," Green said. Green reached an

Head coach Dennis Green's ability to win despite a revolving door at the quarterback position was noteworthy.

agreement with McCombs over the final two years of his contract, which was worth about $5 million.

As members of the team stood solemnly in the back of the Vikings weight room, Green expressed his admiration for the players he had worked with over the past 10 years.

"Some guys who most people never thought would have played in the National Football League, but they were looking for an opportunity," Green said. "Those are the type of players that made up the 10 years that we've been here with the Minnesota Vikings. What we try to do is treat them all the same. We try to give them all an opportunity to reach their goals to reach their dreams to be successful. And that's something I've enjoyed."

Green would resume his head coaching career with the Arizona Cardinals prior to the 2004 season, but he did not come close to making the playoffs in the desert and struggled to build his new team. He was fired after three losing seasons. His legacy remains building a truly competitive team in Minnesota that never quite reached its enormous potential.

THE MATURATION OF RANDALL CUNNINGHAM

He was one of the NFL's marquee players as the quarterback for the Philadelphia Eagles. His highlight film plays featured athletic escapes followed by 65-yard heaves downfield. Cunningham did things on the field that no other quarterback outside of John Elway or Brett Favre could even think of doing.

But all the athletic ability in the world did not make Cunningham a consistent quarterback. His success was tempered by bouts of inaccuracy and his unchecked ego often got in the way. When he parted company with the Eagles following the 1995 season, very few of his teammates were sad to see him leave. He took his ball and went home. Not necessarily because he didn't want to play—he couldn't find anyone who wanted to employ him. With his nose in the air, he stayed at home in Las Vegas and worked at his custom marble and granite business. Not bad work if you can get it, but certainly nothing like the charmed life one leads in the NFL.

The year off did Cunningham a lot of good. It humbled him. When Denny Green and the Vikings came calling and talked about him filling a role as the team's backup quarterback to Brad Johnson for the 1997 season, Cunningham was all ears. He wanted to get back in the game and didn't care if he was no longer one of the elite.

"I know my role here and I'm totally comfortable with that," Cunningham said when he signed with the Vikings. "Brad Johnson is the man here and that's just fine with me. I'll be ready when and if I'm needed."

Cunningham had seen how the other half lived in his year off from the game. He started to realize how good he had had it when he was an NFL player. He might still make mistakes on the field with the Vikings, but he would no longer act as if he was entitled to royal treatment because he was a superstar. He recognized that he had acted like a spoiled child at times and that he was indeed very lucky to be back in the NFL.

Randall Cunningham celebrates a 66-yard touchdown pass to Vikings receiver Cris Carter during an NFC playoff game against the 49ers on January 3, 1998. Dennis Green gave Cunningham another opportunity to show off his athleticism, cannon arm, and experience at a time when his career seemed to be over. Cunningham was brilliant during the Vikings' memorable 15–1 season of 1998.

"I've matured as a person," Cunningham said. "A year away from the game really helped my perspective. I feel like just a regular guy and that's all I want to be. I really appreciate being a part of this team."

Many were skeptical of Cunningham's sudden change in perspective and personality, but he demonstrated through his actions that he was no longer the obnoxious diva he had become with the Eagles. He traded his $3.2 million salary in 1995 for $425,000 with Minnesota in '97. If he had focused on the change in his financial status he would have been miserable, but none of that mattered to the "new" Cunningham. He had a chance to play again and that's all he wanted.

One of Cunningham's biggest supporters turned out to be Johnson, who understood that he would eventually be competing with the former Eagle but didn't let that fact stop the two from working together and enjoying the process quite a bit. Johnson described Cunningham as "helpful and positive," something he never heard from his teammates in Philadelphia.

There was a calmness and peace about Cunningham in Minnesota that never existed when he was with the Eagles. Booed resoundingly by the tough Philly fans in his final years, he was determined to stay within himself with the Vikings.

He knew he had overstayed his welcome in Philadelphia and wished he had asked to be traded a couple of years before he was released. "For eight years, I couldn't do anything wrong there but then it got to the point where it just wasn't working any more," Cunningham said. "But that's not unusual in Philadelphia where guys like Charles Barkley, Mike Schmidt, and Dr. J [Julius Erving] stayed too long and heard about it from fans. That's a good group to be with.

"I was a very loyal guy. I should have asked to be traded but I never did because I wanted to be loyal. It turned out to be the wrong situation but I found the right situation in Minnesota."

Cunningham proved to be a solid backup in 1997, starting three games and completing 44 of 88 passes for 501 yards with eight touchdowns and four interceptions. Not spectacular, but it proved to Green that Cunningham was still viable. The Vikings went 9–7 and made the playoffs as a wild-card team. They upset the Giants 23–22 in the wild-card game before losing 38–22 at San Francisco in the divisional playoffs.

There was clearly quite a bit of disappointment when the season came to an end, but it was also clear that the groundwork had been set for a great 1998 season. Cunningham would compete with Johnson for the starting position during the summer and he once again started the season on the bench.

However, when Johnson broke his leg in the third game of the season, Cunningham came in and did the job more than adequately. While Cunningham never had the quick release of a Dan Marino or Joe Montana, he had a very smooth delivery and the huge Vikings offensive line gave him plenty of time to find open receivers.

He was simply brilliant in his passing and decision making and his play was one of the biggest factors for a team that was 15–1—along with a rookie wide receiver named Randy Moss. The team was simply a juggernaut during the regular season.

Cunningham combined the know-how of an old master while still maintaining his athletic edge. He completed 259 of 425 passes for 3,704 yards with 34 touchdowns and 10 interceptions. He also ran for 132 yards and another touchdown.

It was complete vindication for a player who had been viewed as one of the most spoiled athletes of his generation during his 11 tempestuous seasons in Philadelphia. After battling with team-mates, coaches, and the media on his old team, he took on the persona of elder statesman and played like a leader when his team needed him most.

To paraphrase Winston Churchill, the 1998 season was Cunningham's finest hour.

ESERA COMES OUT

The Vikings found themselves in the middle of a social controversy in 2002 when former defensive lineman Esera Tuaolo announced on HBO's *Real Sports with Bryant Gumbel* that he was gay.

Tuaolo had kept his identity hidden during his playing career, which included five seasons with the Vikings. The former All-Pac-10 player from Oregon played the best football of his career with the Vikings, all the while keeping his identity as a gay man hidden. He loved playing the game of football, but the macho culture of the NFL wouldn't allow him to reveal his lifestyle.

"I wanted to say who I was on many occasions and at times I was tempted," Tuaolo explained in his autobiography, *Alone in the Trenches*. "But I knew that my teammates would not accept it and my career would likely be over."

The locker room was a bastion of antigay jokes and remarks and Tuaolo often participated in the ridicule in order to keep his secret. "I had to keep the dogs off the scent," he explained.

Tuaolo recalled one incident in which teammate John Randle had gotten under the skin of a particularly thin-skinned teammate by saying "You must be gay." Randle was merely trying to get a rise out of the player and wasn't necessarily trying to insult him, but the remarks instigated a full-scale locker room brawl between the two.

"Everybody tried to break it up, including me," Tuaolo said. "John's locker was right next to mine. I tried to pull him off the other guy and got hit in the back of the head. I felt the adrenaline surge of the fight. I also felt tremendous pain. That could have been me getting teased and in a fight."

Vikings head coach Dennis Green called a team meeting after the fight, explaining that someone could have gotten hurt and that would have weakened the team. He described the incident as selfish. "We depend on each other as teammates," Green said. "This is supposed to be a team."

During the midst of Green's talk to put the problem in the past, Tuaolo thought about coming out with his situation and revealing his sexual orientation. "I should have said something like 'I'm gay, so what?'" he said in retrospect.

But Tuaolo kept quiet and the anxiety continued to eat at him.

Tuaolo even went so far as to go out with and sleep with women just

TRIVIA

Who are the only Vikings to be named NFL Offensive Player of the Year?

Find the answers on pages 193–194.

Former Minnesota Vikings player Esera Tuaolo poses after a 2002 interview on HBO's *Real Sports with Bryant Gumbel* during which he revealed his homosexuality.

to keep his teammates at arm's length. He managed to keep his sexual orientation a secret, but he was miserable leading a duplicitous lifestyle.

At the same time, Tuaolo was becoming an accomplished player. After stepping into the Vikings defensive line as a full-time starter in 1995, Tuaolo used his quickness to record 45 tackles, three sacks, one forced fumble, and two fumble recoveries. He played next to John Randle and the Vikings had some of the best interior defensive line play in the league.

Tuaolo was glad to be an important part of the team, but the better he performed the more he feared that his secret would come out. "I was in the limelight and out of the shadows," Tuaolo said. "Those games after a sack, I panicked. Success brought fear. In the off-season I had gone back to Hawaii [his home state]. A larger number of guys knew my secret. There was a possibility one of them could out me."

Such was the state of Tuaolo's life. He was a gifted football player who enjoyed the game, but because he was protecting his

COMMENTS ON TUAOLO FROM NFL PLAYERS

While many of the comments made by NFL players regarding Esera Tuaolo's decision to reveal his sexuality were positive, it would be naïve to come to the conclusion that most players would accept a gay teammate. Those who would condemn it realized that a negative statement would brand them as homophobic and so many of those players just kept their mouths shut.

"I really don't see it as being that big a deal. It might make some people uncomfortable, but to me it's a non-issue."

—Todd Steussie, Tuaolo's former teammate with the
Minnesota Vikings, in *The Herald* (Rock Hill, South Carolina)

"Aww, hell no! I don't want any faggots on my team. I know this might not be what people want to hear, but that's a punk. I don't want any faggots in this locker room."

—Garrison Hearst, San Francisco 49ers running back, in the *Fresno Bee*

"Guys don't assume that their teammates are of a homosexual preference, just because of the nature of what we do. I'm sure it would be a hostile environment, because there are a lot of macho attitudes in the locker room. Who has the prettiest girl? Who drives the biggest car? Who is playing the best? I could see where a person would hide that. That would be one of the toughest environments to come out in."

—Henri Crockett, Tuaolo's former teammate
with the Atlanta Falcons, in the *St. Paul Pioneer Press*

"It really doesn't concern me, because I'm definitely not homophobic. I know that there are homosexuals in every occupation, and with the number of homosexuals out there, I wouldn't doubt there are some in athletics. The odds are, with the number of guys I've played with, I've probably been in the locker room with some.

"We as a culture have to be open-minded to different things and different situations, and that goes for sexuality, religion, and different cultures. Because you come in a locker room like this, there are people who are totally different from me, probably grew up in a totally different environment from me. But it just comes down to being open-minded and being understanding of other people."

—Byron Chamberlain, Tuaolo's former teammate
with the Minnesota Vikings, in the *St. Paul Pioneer Press*

"He would have been eaten alive and he would have been hated for it. Had he come out on a Monday, with Wednesday, Thursday, Friday practices, he'd have never gotten to the other team."

—Sterling Sharpe, Tuaolo's former teammate with the Green Bay Packers, on
HBO's *Real Sports with Bryant Gumbel*. An NFL spokesman, Greg Aiello,
characterized Sharpe's message as "unfortunate and irresponsible." Aiello
went on to declare the NFL a "meritocracy" based on "job performance,"
in Robert Lipsyte's column in *The New York Times*. "And on that basis an
individual's sexual orientation is entirely irrelevant," he said.

"First of all, I'm proud of Esera Tuaolo. By coming out to the world, he did something a lot of guys would never have the guts to do. We were teammates in Green Bay, and I know him pretty well. And now, knowing that he's gay, it doesn't change anything. I don't have any bad feelings about it. To me, it's not that big of a deal. But the reality is, I may be in the minority.

"...A lot of guys would be upset. Particularly because football players shower together. I'm sure a lot of guys are looking back right now and wondering if Tuaolo was checking them out. For many players—and for many heterosexual men in general—it's distressing to know that a guy you're sharing soap with is gay. I have to admit, if I knew an openly gay guy was in the shower, I would not be in a rush to go in there.

"...I'm proud of Tuaolo for standing up for who he is, but I think he made a wise decision in waiting to come out. Football is a masculine, violent sport. There is a lot of emphasis on toughness. As a player, the last thing you want to be portrayed as is 'soft.' Other players wouldn't want to go into battle with him on Sundays, he'd most certainly be treated differently."

—LeRoy Butler, Tuaolo's former teammate
with the Green Bay Packers, in an ESPN.com column

"Most players I know are so confident in their own sexuality they wouldn't care about the gay player two lockers down so long as he acts professionally.

"If a player admitted he was gay, I suspect his teammates wouldn't like it—they'd hate the media circus—but they'd learn to deal with it.

"I wonder whether we could do the same."

—Chris Havel, Green Bay Packers
writer/columnist for Gannett

"Guys wouldn't come out and say [they're gay] and still be playing football now because they would be looked upon differently. They would be ridiculed so much. Even with free speech and free choice and things like that nature in society today, football and the locker room is something different.

"There's an old-school mentality, that if someone wants to come out and say they were [gay] and was still playing, I think he'd have a hard time doing [his] job and focusing."

—Darren Sharper, Green Bay Packers
defensive back, on PackersNews.com

"The whole ordeal about [Tuaolo] coming out shouldn't even be as publicized as it is. Millions of people make that decision every day and don't get glamorized for it. It becomes a problem when you focus on it or when it becomes an issue or the media get involved."

—Vonnie Holliday, Green Bay Packers lineman, on PackersNews.com

"I would accept [a gay player] personally, because we live in a world where we're all sinners and nobody is perfect.

"I'm not one to judge another man. I would accept him, because if I don't, I would say I'm better than that person or looking down on him, but I know I'm not perfect."

—Kabeer Gbaja-Biamila, Green Bay Packers
lineman, on PackersNews.com

"I think he's looking for a lawsuit. If he's gay, he's gay. Who cares? Go on with your life.

"…There's a lot of gay jokes, yeah. You've got a bunch of naked men running around here, it's going to be uncomfortable if one of them is looking at you."
—Luke Petitgout, New York Giants tackle,
in Paul Needell's column in *The Star-Ledger* (Newark, New Jersey)

"I think you respect their boundaries and respect what they are and who they are. It's all about how you are with yourself—if you're not comfortable with yourself and who you are, then you may be uncomfortable."
—Richie Anderson, New York Jets running back,
in Paul Needell's column in *The Star-Ledger* (Newark, New Jersey)

"Hey buddy, here's the deal. You know I disagree with it and I believe God forbids it, but I love you like a brother. If you can handle me not agreeing with your lifestyle…then we can be friends."
—Craig Sauer, on what he told ex-teammate Tuaolo
upon hearing he was gay, on HBO's *Real Sports with Bryant Gumbel*

"I could see coming out to make a statement if the league had a rule that gays couldn't play or something like that. But that's not the case. So just shut up."
—Marshall Faulk, St. Louis Rams running back,
speaking on the subject in general in *Playboy* magazine

"If we had a guy who was gay on this team, it's none of my business what he does outside of the locker room. My business is my business, and his business is his business. I wouldn't treat him any different. Definitely not."
—Greg Biekert, Minnesota Vikings linebacker, in the *St. Paul Pioneer Press*

"For so long I've felt the isolation of always being the only gay football player that's out there. Esera will have a life, children, and a partner, things I never have had. I felt regret, but also a sense of validation and freedom, and a relief that the world was finally changing."
—David Kopay, gay ex-NFL player,
in Robert Lipsyte's column in *The New York Times*

Quotes compiled by Outsports.com

identity from anyone connected with the business, he lived in constant fear and was unable to enjoy his success.

Tuaolo got hurt in the last game of the 1995 season when he tore his Achilles tendon in a game on the rock-hard turf at Cincinnati's Riverfront Stadium.

He had surgery and rehabbed during the winter and came back to play in 1996, but not at the level that either he or the team expected. He moved on to the Jacksonville Jaguars in 1997, the Falcons in 1998, and closed out his career with the Panthers in 1999.

The '98 season brought him back to Minnesota when the Vikings hosted the Falcons in the NFC championship game.

TRIVIA

In what years did Dennis Green coach, and what was his coaching record?

Find the answers on pages 193–194.

Tuaolo's teammates on the Falcons came to him for scouting reports on his former teammates. In particular, he was effective at providing tips on what moves work against All-Pro offensive linemen Todd Steussie and Randall McDaniel. Tuaolo also got quite a bit of playing time as a run stuffer and in goal-line situations.

Going back to the Metrodome for a confrontation with the 15–1 Vikings in a game that would decide the NFC championship and give the winner a spot in the Super Bowl was thrilling for Tuaolo, but he was miffed when only one of his former teammates, running back Robert Smith, came over and said hello to him before the game. Nobody else even acknowledged him with a nod or a hello.

Tuaolo told his Falcons teammates of the snub and they agreed that it was cold. It only added fuel to their passion. Atlanta head coach Dan Reeves and his players defied the odds and upset the Vikings 30–27 in overtime.

After one more season, Tuaolo's career would come to an end. He decided to reveal his sexual preference in 2002 to help others who were caught in their own identity crisis. He has gone on to become a successful musician and motivational speaker. He was embraced by the gay community, including actress/comedienne Rosie O'Donnell.

The NFL's reaction was mixed, with more negative than positive remarks. Former teammates Sterling Sharpe and Cris Carter said that players would likely "take out" a gay teammate in practice and that he would not be able to play in a game. San Francisco running back Garrison Hearst said he did not want to play with any "faggots."

TRIVIA

Which two Vikings were named All-Pro in 1995?

Find the answers on pages 193–194.

But former teammates Don Davey (Green Bay and Jacksonville) and Jeff Novak (Jacksonville) called Tuaolo in support and friendship. Even former Packers defensive line coach Greg Blache sent an email saying he was proud of the courage Tuaolo displayed in making his revelation and that he was glad he was finally happy.

The NFL's culture makes it difficult for any player to consider coming out in the middle of their career. But the league's power structure is committed to diversity training and brought Tuaolo in to get his opinion. Considering that former commissioner Paul Tagliabue's son Drew is openly gay, the league's progressiveness in the area is not surprising.

THE AGONY OF DEFEAT

SUPER BOWL IV: THE VIKINGS RUN INTO AN AFL STEAMROLLER

It was supposed to be a coronation. Instead it turned out to be a funeral.

The Vikings had pillaged the NFL in 1969, winning 12 of 14 regular-season games and handling the Los Angeles Rams and Cleveland Browns in the playoffs. The 27–7 win over Cleveland was notable because it sent the Vikings to their first Super Bowl appearance against the Kansas City Chiefs and it cemented their reputation as a skilled, powerful, and nasty team that dominated nearly every time they took the field.

The Browns never stood a chance in the last NFL championship game ever played after Vikings quarterback Joe Kapp scrambled out of the pocket and blasted through the Cleveland defense. Shedding tacklers like a fullback, Kapp scored on a seven-yard run to open the scoring.

The Vikings took heart from Kapp's usual machismo and rolled to an easy 27–7 win. Despite playing on a frozen field at Metropolitan Stadium, the Vikings looked comfortable and determined. Kapp connected with wide receiver Gene Washington on a 75-yard touchdown pass. The Browns never knew what hit them.

"That was our team playing our way," Kapp said. "Nothing was going to stop us on that day and we made our points early. Our defense was simply too tough. We played with an attitude and the

Browns were not going to be able to match us in our ballpark on that day. It was a game—and a feeling I will always remember."

The Vikings were clearly the NFL's best team. Then it was on to Super Bowl IV and a chance for their first championship in their ninth year of existence.

Minnesota was expected to dominate the AFL's Chiefs and make a statement in Super Bowl IV. In addition to playing for the championship of professional football, they were playing to regain pride for the National Football League in the last battle ever with the American Football League. (The merger had been effected in 1966 and this would be the last time the AFL would take the field. The following year, the league became the American Football Conference and part of the NFL.)

TRIVIA

Who has caught the most passes in Vikings history?

Find the answers on pages 193–194.

The year before, the Baltimore Colts had lost Super Bowl III to the New York Jets and that defeat had wounded the pride of Pete Rozelle and everyone connected with the NFL. Head coach Bud Grant knew he was fighting for a lot more than just a Super Bowl title and so did the Vikings players. They were not only expected to beat the Chiefs, but to grind them into submission.

The Chiefs had a clever quarterback in Len Dawson and a quotable coach in Hank Stram, but they did not appear to have the all-around talent to compete with the Vikings for 60 minutes. A big play here or there? Sure. But the Vikings' vicious front four of Carl Eller, Alan Page, Gary Larsen, and Jim Marshall were expected to impose a fearful beating on the Chiefs offensive line, which was big and strong, but nowhere near as athletic as Minnesota's front four.

But a funny thing had happened the year before when the Jets beat the Colts in Super Bowl III. The entire American Football League had become emboldened by the victory. When the Jets won, it was good for the Chiefs, Raiders, Chargers, and Patriots. So while the Vikings might have been playing to win back the NFL's

THE OTHER SIDE OF THE COIN: LEN DAWSON EXPLAINS KANSAS CITY'S RESOLVE IN SUPER BOWL IV

We were respectful of the Vikings and we knew they had a great year. But we had improved significantly. We studied films and I was very confident we could move the ball and score on them. My roommate was [safety] Johnny Robinson and he told me he didn't think the Vikings would score on the defense. Both the offense and the defense were extremely confident that the game would turn out much better than the first time we had been in the Super Bowl.

I had an extremely difficult week when the story broke about my name and phone number being in the possession of a known gambler. It was a national story because it was the week of the Super Bowl and it was very distracting. But I never let it bother my concentration because I knew I had done nothing wrong.

At one point when I was being interrogated by the officials, I actually fell asleep. You can't do that if you're nervous about having done something wrong or illegal. I knew I had nothing to worry about. [Dawson was completely exonerated from any wrongdoing.]

As the week moved along, I thought we had another advantage over the Vikings. We had been there before and we knew what to expect. The Vikings had to deal with the press, their families and friends who wanted tickets. It was their first time in that position. We had been through that situation before against Green Bay and the experience made the second go-round a lot easier. We had to deal with our families and other distractions, but it did not drain our energy. I don't think it bothered us the way it did the Vikings.

In our preparation we felt we would find a way to move the ball on them both through the air and the ground. We thought we could beat their corners with [wide receiver] Otis Taylor and we also thought our offensive line could have a very good day.

It turned out that we were able to do just that. I got plenty of protection that day from my great offensive line. We moved the ball well throughout the first half, but they were able to keep us out of the end zone and three times we had to settle for field goals. However, late in the second quarter,

Mike Garrett ran the ball in and we had a 16–0 lead that we took into the locker room at halftime. That's the play that you still see on NFL Films, the one where [head coach] Hank [Stram] keeps yelling "Sixty-five toss power trap, sixty-five toss power trap."

We were feeling great at that point, and even though the Vikings scored in the third quarter, I knew we had control of the game. A few minutes later, the Vikings came at me in an all-out blitz and I had called for a very quick pass to [wide receiver] Otis Taylor. It was just a little out pattern, but it was all that Otis needed and he scored on a 46-yard play. It seems that nearly every big play I had that year involved Otis. In the playoff win over the Jets, he made a big catch that helped turn the game in our favor. In the AFL championship game against the Raiders, he did the same thing. It was only fitting that he made the most significant play in the Super Bowl.

After that play, I knew it was over. We didn't need to score another point because our defense played so well. Willie Lanier, Bobby Bell, Curley Culp, and Buck Buchanan. They were just too strong for the Minnesota offensive line. The only thing that could have turned the game in their favor was if we started making awful mistakes on offense and it just wasn't going to happen on that day.

To play so many years and finally get your first world championship, it was a tremendous feeling. A lot of critics out there thought the Jets' victory the year before over the Colts had been a fluke win for the AFL but we proved it was not. It was great for the AFL and great for the city and people of Kansas City. Personally, I loved the feeling of being a champion.

pride, the Chiefs were playing to reconfirm what the Jets had done the year before.

"We blustered a lot before the game and thought we were going to win," Kapp said. "We could see they were a good team when we watched them on tape and had some good athletes. But we didn't think they could stay with us. We thought we were going to be Super Bowl champions when we took the field."

But the Chiefs were a confident group themselves and did not believe the oddsmakers who had made the Vikings a two-touchdown favorite to win the game. Their self-confidence was borne out in the opening quarter when the Vikings could not

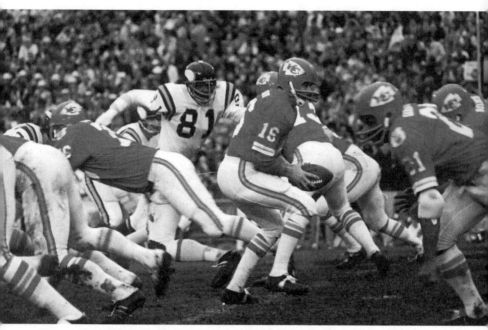

Kansas City Chiefs quarterback Len Dawson turns around to hand the ball off to running back Mike Garrett in Super Bowl IV on January 11, 1970. Dawson's clever play-action fakes left the Vikings on their heels.

move the ball. The offensive line, led by center Mick Tinglehoff, could not get any push against Curley Culp and Buck Buchanan. It became a punt fest for the Vikings.

While the Minnesota defense was not giving in, the Chiefs found a way to get across midfield and give the Chiefs three field goal opportunities. Jan Stenerud made all three kicks and Kansas City's 9–0 lead got stretched to 16–0 when Mike Garrett ran the ball five yards into the end zone on a play that Stram made famous because he was miced for NFL Films. He called it "65 toss power trap" and was giddy with excitement when Garrett ran into the end zone.

As thrilled as Stram was, Grant was pained by the turn of events. Not only was his team getting beaten by its AFL foe, it was getting taken apart. There was no rousing halftime speech—it wouldn't have helped and it was not his style—but an emphasis on finishing blocks and getting back to basics.

Minnesota had a bit of a surge early in the third quarter when they forced a punt and drove 69 yards in 10 plays to get on the board. Running back Dave Osborn got the call and powered the ball into the end zone from four yards out.

Momentum had changed and the Vikings had new life on the sidelines. "I looked into our eyes when we got back on the sideline and there was a different feeling," Kapp said. "We had our confidence back—at least for an instant. We thought we were going to turn things around and win the game."

But the Chiefs took care of that, moving from their own 18 to the Vikings 46. Then disaster struck when Dawson hit speedy wide receiver Otis Taylor with a five-yard hitch pass; Taylor then ran through Minnesota defensive back Earsell Mackbee. Taylor ran down the sidelines, evaded a tackle from safety Karl Kassulke and scored the touchdown that ended the Vikings' hopes.

"As quickly as we had gotten some momentum, that's how quickly we lost it," said Kapp. "The same energy I felt just a few moments earlier was gone."

The Vikings had appeared unbeatable before the start of the game but were shattered. They came back to roll through the 1970 regular season with a 12–2 record, but that postseason failure had imprinted itself on the Vikings psyche. It came to the fore when they lost at home to the 49ers in the playoffs and it would happen again many times thereafter.

VIKINGS HELP STEELERS BEGIN DYNASTY

The Vikings established themselves as an NFL power by combining a physical defense with a resourceful and creative offense along with excellence on special teams.

Bud Grant's team always had plenty of confidence every time it took the field, but the Super Bowl experience was one it could never master. On the face of things, they appeared to be meeting their equals when they faced the Steelers in Super Bowl IX at Tulane Stadium in New Orleans, but in actuality they were in way over their heads.

The Vikings had finished 10–4 during the regular season and then dispatched the St. Louis Cardinals with ease in the divisional playoffs. The 30–14 win was never in doubt as Fran Tarkenton moved his team through the St. Louis defense with ease. Their 14–10 win over the Rams in the NFC championship was more of a struggle, but the Vikings were thought to have a bit of an edge against the Steelers because they had been in two earlier Super Bowls, including Super Bowl VIII against the Dolphins the previous season.

Nobody knew it at the time, but the Steelers were about to become one of the legendary teams in NFL history. This was their first appearance in the Super Bowl and it was expected that Terry Bradshaw, Franco Harris, and Mean Joe Greene might be a bit nervous playing for their first league title.

Fat chance. The Steelers were about as nervous as Mount Rushmore and just as tough to move. They had won the AFC Central with a 10–3–1 record and had beaten Buffalo and Oakland in the AFC playoffs with ease. The 24–13 victory over the Raiders was particularly noteworthy because it came in Oakland and they were able to establish a running attack against a nasty Oakland defense.

Instead it was the Vikings who had a case of the nerves, turning the ball over five times. The Steelers emerged with a 16–6 win that was not as close as the score indicated.

Tarkenton and the Vikings offense felt as though they had been battered around by the Pittsburgh Steel Curtain defense. They were held to 119 total yards and had just 47 plays compared to the Steelers' 73. The most astounding number in the game may have been the difference in the two teams' rushing totals. Harris and Rocky Bleier kept pounding away from start to finish and the Steelers finished the game with 249 rushing yards. The Vikings turned to Chuck Foreman and Dave Osborn and did not get the same results. They ran for 17 yards as Greene, Ernie Holmes, Dwight White, and L.C. Greenwood punished the Vikings offensive line and the two ball carriers.

The game was scoreless into the second quarter and the Vikings had the ball at their own 10. Tarkenton tried to pitch the ball to Osborn, but the ball never reached Osborn's midsection and sailed into the end zone. Tarkenton fell on it for a Pittsburgh safety.

The errant pitch perplexed Tarkenton. "My arm hit something," Tarkenton recalled. "Someone's arm or leg, I was never sure. I thought I got it back good enough to get it to Dave, but he said it never touched him."

The Vikings defense was not allowing the Steelers to do much when they had the ball, and with five minutes remaining in the first half, Minnesota mounted a serious drive. Tarkenton had driven the Vikes 55 yards to the Pittsburgh 25. Tarkenton hit Foreman with a 17-yard pass over the middle and an interference penalty against Steelers defensive back Mel Blount on a pass to wideout John Gilliam keyed the drive.

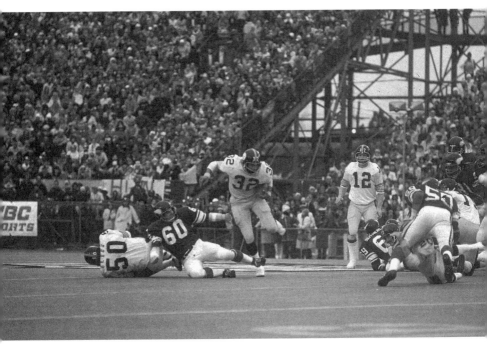

Pittsburgh Steelers running back Franco Harris rumbles for extra yardage during Super Bowl IX on January 12, 1975. Harris gave the Steelers a credible running game; Vikings defensive tackle Alan Page said his squad had faced—and stopped—better backs during the season, but for some reason they couldn't slow down Harris.

Tarkenton had the Vikings in position to take the lead with a field goal before halftime, but he was looking for more. He fired the ball to Gilliam at the 10, but the receiver could not control the ball and it bounded into the air and Blount brought it in at the goal line.

On the second half kickoff, Pittsburgh's Roy Gerela slipped as he got into his kick and the ball bounced to the 28. Bill Brown picked it up, but he fumbled it and the Steelers recovered at the Minnesota 30.

The blood was in the water and the Steelers went after it like sharks. Pittsburgh succeeded with its vaunted ground attack. After Bleier was stopped, Harris went left for 24 yards to give the Steelers first-and-goal. Following a loss of three yards on first down, Harris took a power sweep nine yards for the first touchdown.

The Vikings trailed 9–0, but they were still clearly in the game. However, after getting stopped on their own 37, their next possession was marred by Greene's interception of a Tarkenton pass.

The Steelers returned the favor when Harris fumbled two minutes into the fourth quarter and Paul Krause recovered for Minnesota at the Pittsburgh 47. Another interference call on a pass to Gilliam—this time by Mike Wagner—gave the Vikings first-and-goal at the 5. Minnesota could not take advantage as the normally sure-handed Foreman lost the ball at the 7.

The Vikings defense rose up and stopped the Steelers before they could register a first down and Bobby Walden punted from his own end zone. At least he attempted to. Linebacker Matt Blair came racing in and cleanly blocked Walden's punt. Resourceful Terry Brown recovered it in the end zone. But there was to be no comeback. Fred Cox missed the ensuing extra point and Bradshaw led the Steelers on an 11-play, 66-yard drive. Bradshaw concluded the drive by hitting tight end Larry Brown with a four-yard touchdown pass.

When the Vikings' defensive unit left the field for the last time, with less than a minute remaining, Page slammed his helmet to the ground in a gesture of disgust. "I didn't think I'd need it anymore," explained the tackle.

"It didn't bother me so much that we lost, but that we had some players who didn't want to win," Page said. "Franco Harris is a good running back, but we have faced others who were just as good or better. We just weren't good enough to beat them."

That Pittsburgh touchdown gave the Steelers their 10-point margin and a Wagner interception officially closed the door on Minnesota's chances.

Turnovers were the story of the game for the Vikings. One led to a safety, one to a touchdown, and three others stopped Minnesota drives.

Grant was frustrated at his team's play in their third chance to win the Super Bowl. "It was not a good game," Grant said. "Neither team got here playing that kind of football. There were turnovers, missed field goals, a blocked punt, and penalties. They took advantage of those plays more than we did.

"Our defense really played well. We really had a chance to win, but they were able to deflect passes and make plays. On one of those picks, Stu Voigt was wide open but Greene picked it off. It was frustrating."

It was just as painful for his players and the Vikings' long-suffering fans. The Vikings had lost Super Bowls to the Chiefs, Dolphins, and Steelers and was getting the reputation of a team that could not win the big one. While it might have been a harsh assessment, playing consistently and well was simply not enough. The team needed to validate itself with a championship.

SUPER BOWL XI: THE RAIDERS LOWER THE BOOM ON THE VIKINGS

The Vikings and the Raiders were on a collision course throughout the 1976 season. While the Vikings were the dominant team in the NFC with an 11–2–1 record, the Raiders were even more impressive in the AFC with a 13–1 record.

However, Oakland was far from invulnerable and it took a couple of questionable officials' calls and a 14-point rally late in the fourth quarter to escape with a 24–21 victory over the Patriots in the first round of the AFC playoffs.

The Vikings had no such issues in their first-round meeting with the wild-card Washington Redskins. Minnesota toyed with Washington, building a 35–6 lead after three quarters before

TRIVIA

Who is the Vikings all-time leading scorer?

Find the answers on pages 193–194.

calling off the dogs and coasting in with a 35–20 victory.

It was the kind of game that warmed head coach Bud Grant's heart. Chuck Foreman (105 yards) and Brent McClanahan (101) both eclipsed the century mark while Fran Tarkenton threw three touchdown passes, including two to rookie wide receiver Sammy White.

The defense frustrated Washington at every turn and Redskins quarterback Billy Kilmer simply could not get anything going until the game had been decided in the fourth quarter.

"This was a demonstration of what emotion is in a football game," said Grant. "The Vikings were a very emotional team in that game. Washington had played very emotional football the past several weeks just to get into the playoffs and they simply ran out of it. We made some big plays because we played with emotion and they didn't."

The Vikings moved forward to the NFC championship, where they faced a Los Angeles Rams team that had lost in that game the two previous years. Head coach Chuck Knox had his team fired up and playing its best football, but the Vikings' opportunistic nature and superiority on special teams allowed them to emerge with a 24–13 victory and a trip to Pasadena to play in the Super Bowl against the Raiders. Oakland had dispatched an undermanned Pittsburgh team—neither Franco Harris nor Rocky Bleier played due to injuries—with ease in a 24–7 victory.

In the Vikings win, Minnesota's Nate Allen blocked an early Tom Dempsey field goal attempt in the first quarter and Bobby Bryant picked up the ball and ran 90 yards for the opening touchdown of the game.

"Nate made a beautiful block on the play and the ball just bounced up to me," said Bryant. "It just bounced right up into my hands and I took off. I never had a bounce work out so perfectly. The big question was whether I would make it 90 yards down the field without collapsing."

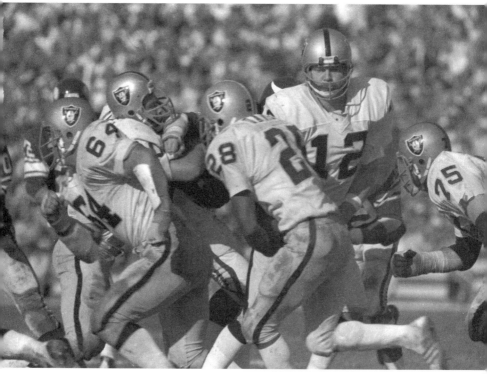

Oakland Raiders quarterback Ken Stabler (No. 12) hands off the ball to team-mate Clarence Davis during first-half action in Super Bowl XI on January 9, 1977.

The special teams were far from done. All-purpose linebacker Matt Blair blocked a Rusty Jackson boot in the second quarter when the Rams punter dropped the snap from center, and the Vikings took possession at the Rams 8. Four plays later, Fred Cox kicked a 25-yard field goal.

Once again, Grant pointed to his team's emotional edge. He credited his team's younger players for bringing more exuberance to the team. Grant was hoping that emotional edge would play a role in the Super Bowl matchup with the Raiders and finally get the team over the hump in the big game, but disappointment was to haunt them one more time.

Going into this game, many of the media wise guys pointed to this as a battle of losers. The Vikings had lost their three previous

Super Bowl appearances, while the Raiders had dropped Super Bowl II to the Packers and had lost in the AFL or AFC championship game five times after that defeat. Words like "gag" and "choke" regularly accompanied both teams as the pregame hype built.

One area where Raiders coach John Madden knew his team had an advantage was in size and strength in the pit. Specifically, his offensive line was much bigger than the Vikings' Purple Gang up front. Huge offensive tackle Art Shell outweighed Carl Eller by 40 pounds and guard Gene Upshaw also had a significant advantage over Alan Page. With both of his studs neutralized, Grant's defense got pushed around.

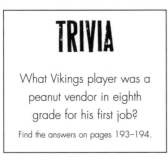

TRIVIA

What Vikings player was a peanut vendor in eighth grade for his first job?

Find the answers on pages 193–194.

Raiders quarterback Ken Stabler had his choice of weapons. He could hand the ball to Clarence Davis or Mark van Eeghen in the backfield or throw it to Fred Biletnikoff, Dave Casper, and Cliff Branch. Stabler was masterful as the Raiders built a 16–0 halftime lead that left the Vikings teetering on the brink of their fourth consecutive Super Bowl loss.

In the first 30 minutes, the Raiders defense allowed 27 rushing yards and 39 passing yards. The Vikings had gotten beyond midfield twice, but their inability to move the ball once they got there proved to be decisive.

Minnesota actually had a great opportunity to dictate the pace of the game early when their special teams made a huge and unexpected play. Oakland punter Ray Guy took the field in a scoreless first quarter, never having had a punt blocked in his illustrious career. Minnesota linebacker Fred McNeill put a stop to that streak when he knifed in and smothered Guy's punt and fell on it in on the Oakland 3.

The Raiders were calm and confident despite the poor field position and linebacker Phil Villapiano forced a McClanahan fumble that was recovered by Raiders linebacker Willie Hall. Oakland took over and did not allow the Vikings to have any serious scoring opportunities until the second half.

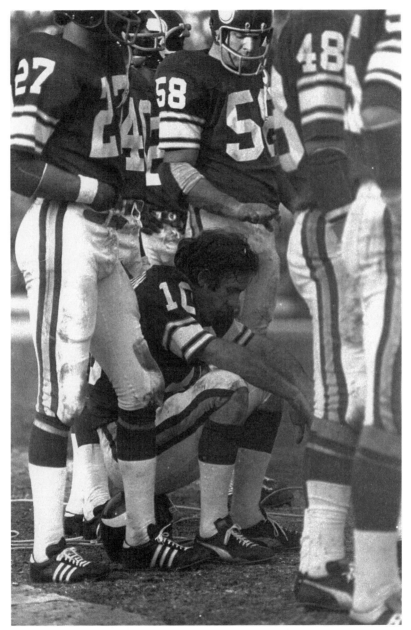

Minnesota quarterback Fran Tarkenton, finishing his third Super Bowl without a victory, sits on his helmet during the final minutes as his team goes down to defeat again, this time against the Oakland Raiders.

THE OTHER SIDE OF THE COIN: BIG COACH REACHES HIS GOAL

For more than two decades, John Madden has been pro football's preeminent television analyst. At his best, he is knowledgeable, entertaining, and insightful. At his worst, he is loud and repetitive.

A couple of generations of football fans know Madden from his work on television. But he made his bones as a coach, and his 10-year run with the Raiders was spectacular. He compiled a 103–32–7 record in regular-season games, and his .759 career winning percentage is the highest in the history of pro football among coaches who have won 100 games or more—including Vince Lombardi, George Halas, Don Shula, and Curly Lambeau.

But going into the 1976 playoffs, there was plenty of heat on Madden and the Raiders. They had won the AFC West with a spectacular 13–1 record, losing only to the Patriots during the regular season. They were 1–3 against the Steelers in postseason games during the 1970s, and Madden was determined not to let Pittsburgh get the best of him again.

But before taking on the Steelers, the Raiders had a rematch with the Patriots, who had administered a 48–17 demolition in the fourth game of the season. New England was a very confident team despite having to go across country and play in Oakland. The Patriots played an outstanding game and built a 21–10 lead in the fourth quarter behind the play of quarterback Steve Grogan, running back Sam "Bam" Cunningham (Randall Cunningham's older brother), and tight end Russ Francis. However, running back Mark van Eeghen and quarterback Ken Stabler scored on short touchdown runs to allow the Raiders to escape.

A key roughing the passer penalty that was called on nose tackle Ray "Sugar Bear" Hamilton aided the Raiders. The call on a third-and-18 play in the final drive gave the Raiders a first down at the New England 13 and Stabler was able to win the game with his one-yard run.

Oakland followed that with a 24–7 win over the Steelers. Pittsburgh was hampered by injuries to running backs Franco Harris and Rocky Bleier and the Raiders held Chuck Noll's team in check without much of a problem.

Immediately after this game, Madden started making preparations for the Super Bowl. Even though he had never taken his team there before, he had learned that taking care of the "distractions" prior to arriving at the Super Bowl site in Pasadena was extremely important.

Madden had coached in four Pro Bowls—earning that spot as the losing coach in the AFC championship game—and had heard of the many problems that players from the Super Bowl teams had endured.

"I was hanging out with guys who knew what they liked and what they didn't like about the Super Bowl, guys who knew what they thought was important and unimportant," Madden said. "One of those guys was Jake Scott, the Dolphins cornerback. He had been angered by the team's policy of not allowing him to bring his mother—when other players could bring their wives."

Madden wanted to avoid the distractions of problems with tickets, accommodations, and dealing with the media. With two weeks between games, Madden wanted his players to use the first week to rid themselves of distractions. "You each get to buy 30 tickets, but I suggest you get rid of them before we go to L.A. next week," Madden said. "That way nobody will be bothering you next week about tickets. If you don't have any, you don't have any."

As for accommodations, Madden remembered how insulted Scott had felt when the Dolphins didn't allow him to bring his mother. "In addition to your room at the team hotel, we'll arrange for a guest of your choice to go to Los Angeles and have a room at the hotel where our front-office people will be staying," Madden said.

Madden also had advice for his team on the media. Instead of dreading the interview sessions that the league required players to attend, Madden gave them a different perspective. "You're going to get more publicity than you've ever gotten in your life," Madden said. "Have fun with it and enjoy yourselves."

Madden was successful in removing all the normal pre–Super Bowl distractions and his players were able to start working on his game plan at practice the week of the game. He didn't give it to them earlier because he didn't want them to break their normal game week routine or possibly get stale.

The Wednesday practice four days before the game was not a good one and Madden was concerned. However, the next day was a different story. The team was sharp, especially Stabler.

"Kenny had the best practice I've ever seen a quarterback have," Madden recalled. "We threw one-on-one, with one defensive back covering one receiver. We threw what we called 'skeleton,' seven against seven [without the four offensive linemen and the four defensive linemen]. And we threw 'team,' the entire 11 on offense against the 11 on defense.

"For about two hours, Kenny threw over 100 passes and only one pass hit the ground. He completed every other pass he threw, and the one incompletion was a ball that Dave Casper got his hands on it and should have caught it. One incomplete pass in two hours. I had never seen anything like that and I knew we were sharp. When we had another great practice Friday, I knew we would win this game as long as I didn't screw up."

Madden was so confident that he went up to owner Al Davis and told him that the Raiders could not lose. "We're going to kill 'em," Madden said to his boss. "I just know we are going to kill them tomorrow."

Davis was a bit taken aback. "No, no John, don't talk like that," Davis said. "Don't ever talk like that before a game, you know better than that."

Madden was thinking of Davis's warning on the Raiders' third possession. When they were forced to punt for the second time, Vikings linebacker Fred McNeill blocked Ray Guy's punt. It was the only time Guy had ever had a punt blocked. When McNeill fell on it at the Oakland 3-yard line, Madden was worried.

After Chuck Foreman ran to the 2, Raiders linebacker Phil Villapiano hit running back Brent McClanahan on the point of the ball and forced a fumble. Willie Hall recovered at the Raiders 1.

That play turned the game in the Raiders favor. They built a commanding 19–0 lead and the Vikings never got in sync. While the Vikings were suffering in their locker room, the Raiders were celebrating in the other. Both teams had come into the game with monkeys on their backs and the Raiders had gotten rid of theirs.

A great weight had been lifted off Madden's shoulders. His team had finally won the big one and that win would ultimately allow him to begin one of the most successful broadcasting careers in the history of television.

In the final 30 minutes, the Raiders stretched the lead to 19–0 before Tarkenton had a chance to get back into the game. He benefited from two Oakland penalties—running into the kicker by Ted Hendricks and defensive holding by Neal Colzie—and hit White with an eight-yard touchdown pass.

The Raiders were unable to do much on their next possession and it appeared the Vikings might get back in the game when Tarkenton moved the team to the Oakland 37 in eight plays. With Ted Hendricks bearing down on him quickly, Tarkenton fired a pass in the flat to Foreman. Hall intercepted the ball at the Oakland 30 and ran it 16 yards. After a 48-yard pass from Stabler to Biletnikoff, short-yardage specialist Pete Banaszak pounded into the end zone from the 2-yard line for his second touchdown of the game.

The Raiders were clearly in charge with a 26–7 lead and they removed all doubt on the next series. With Tarkenton throwing five straight, he moved the Vikings to the Raiders 28. Tarkenton went to the air again on the next play and legendary cornerback Willie Brown read Tarkenton's eyes the whole way. "Old Man Willie" picked off the pass and ran 75 yards down the sideline for Oakland's final touchdown.

Stu Voigt caught a late touchdown pass from backup quarterback Bob Lee in the game's final seconds to make the final margin 32–14.

The Raiders were clearly the superior team and Tarkenton gave the champions their due. "We had the emotion we needed," Tarkenton said. "But you have to make the plays to keep it going. We made one play, but we couldn't make any others besides the blocked punt. The Raiders played extremely well and we played badly."

Through the 2006 season, the Vikings have not been back. Their 0–4 Super Bowl record leaves them tied with the Buffalo Bills at the bottom of the Super Bowl composite standings. Fans of both teams are hoping the two will meet in the big game—thereby assuring one of these teams of finally winning the big one.

THE WRONG SIDE OF THE LAW

A SMORGASBORD OF INDISCRETIONS

The Vikings are a well-named organization. The original Vikings were Scandinavian warriors who conducted vicious and cruel raids and were dreaded by their enemies.

When general manager Bert Rose found that nickname and recommended it to the Vikings board of directors in 1961, he thought it was the perfect nickname for the team. Not only were ancient Vikings victorious warriors, but also there were many Nordic descendants in the Minneapolis–St. Paul metropolitan area. The board of directors approved Rose's suggestion and the name was well received in the area.

However, the players have often fit the profile of their ancient counterparts. The NFL has a long history of police blotter notoriety, but the Vikings are among the leaders when it comes to off-the-field troubles.

From the infamous Love Boat party on Lake Minnetonka during the Vikings' bye week in the 2005 season to 13 DUI incidents in a four-year span from 1987–90, the Vikings have been far from the disciplined team off the field that Bud Grant envisioned for the franchise when he demanded decorum and soldier-straight posture when the team stood for the national anthem.

While Grant had the kind of military self-discipline that he demanded from his players, the same could not have been said about all coaches that followed him, particularly Dennis Green and his staff.

Here are just a few of the incidents that took place under Green's watchful eye that were pointed out by investigative reporters Jeff Benedict and Don Yaeger in their book *Pros and Cons—The Criminals Who Play in the NFL.*

November 30, 1992. Defensive lineman James Harris was arrested and charged with fifth-degree assault after Bloomington police were dispatched to his home on a 911 violence call. He pleaded guilty 15 days later.

TRIVIA

In what year did Leroy Hoard score nine receiving touchdowns as a pro?

Find the answers on pages 193–194.

October 6, 1993. Running back Keith Henderson was arrested for raping a woman shortly after being cut by the Vikings. That was not his only incident as he was convicted of raping three women in an eight-month span. He was sentenced to six months in jail and 10 years probation.

July 20, 1995. Linebacker Broderick Thomas was caught with a handgun while at Houston International Airport. Charges were dropped.

December 29, 1995. Defensive end James Harris was arrested for beating his wife, a felony assault charge. He pleaded guilty less than a month later and was sentenced to 10 days in the Hennepin County Adult Correction Facility.

March 8, 1996. Defensive back Corey Fuller was arrested for domestic violence and resisting an officer with violence. He pleaded no contest on April 15 of that year. He received a suspended sentence and was placed on probation for one year.

May 7, 1996. Defensive end Fernando Smith was arrested for failing to make court-ordered child support payments. Despite earning $712,499 in salary from the Vikings and receiving a $500,000 signing bonus, Smith had not made any payments to support his daughter. He had previously been convicted of a felony for carrying a concealed weapon in Michigan.

Onterrio Smith, who called himself the 2003 S.O.D. ("steal of the draft"), celebrates after a one-yard touchdown run in a preseason game against the Jacksonville Jaguars. With his infamous "Whizzinator" incident, Smith was one of many players to make the police blotter as a Viking.

June 29, 1997. Safety Orlando Thomas was arrested and charged with starting a riot outside a tavern in Crowley, South Carolina.

October 14, 1997. Center Jeff Christy and tight end Greg DeLong pleaded guilty to carelessly operating a watercraft after being arrested for boating under the influence of alcohol.

January 3, 1998. Wide receiver Chris Walsh was arrested for drunk driving while returning home from a playoff game. He pleaded guilty to careless driving and was sentenced to 30 days in jail. The judge stayed the jail time.

But it wasn't just the players on the Vikings who got into trouble during the Green era. The coach and two of his assistants were also on the wrong end of several incidents embarrassing to the organization.

In early 1992, Green hired Richard Solomon to be his defensive coach. Solomon was Green's former teammate and roommate during his college career at Iowa, but he did not have any pro coaching experience.

After being hired by the team, Solomon was provided with temporary housing at a Bloomington hotel. Providing temporary housing for players and coaches in transition was standard procedure for the Vikings and other teams around the league.

A few weeks after Solomon moved into the hotel, a Vikings official received word that Solomon was making unwanted sexual advances toward a female employee of the facility. Those reports continued for several months.

Then the woman reported that Solomon's verbal harassment escalated to physical assault. The woman, who was in sales with the hotel, did not want to jeopardize her position. *Pros and Cons* stated the woman made her reports to team director of operations Dan Endy, who dutifully took notes and then apprised team vice president Jeff Diamond of the situation.

When Endy came into Diamond's office to report the employee's charge that Solomon had physically harassed her, Diamond had the feeling that the assistant coach had done something again, saying "What did he do now?"

But it wasn't just Solomon who was attempting to use his status and authority to take advantage of attractive women. A

141

Minneapolis hotel sales representative reported that Green was asking her to meet him for breakfast at 6:00 AM every Tuesday during the regular season and would conclude those sessions by kissing her on the lips.

The woman was afraid that failing to meet Green for breakfast could have a huge impact on her employer. The Vikings often rented more than 100 rooms per weekend, even during the off-season.

Endy reported Green's alleged behavior to Diamond just like he had in the case of Solomon. Neither of the female employees had asked him to take it to Vikings upper management. As a result, Endy risked hurting his relationship with the coaching staff by reporting their stories.

Endy was proactive because he was afraid a scandal could hit the news media. From his understanding of the events, it would be headline material if it ever went public and Endy felt the team would be right to fire him if he knew something had happened and he had sat on the information. Endy simply wanted to make sure all his i's were dotted and his t's were crossed.

But by taking his actions, Endy was viewed in a negative light by president Roger Headrick and Green. As a result, Endy was fired after the season. Endy was given a severance package of $75,000 by the Vikings and agreed not to talk about the details of his dismissal.

The Vikings organization knew that it had a problem that it had to address. They held a mandatory sexual harassment seminar in May 1993 to educate everyone within the organization on the subject. But shortly after the seminar, a Vikings intern reported that Solomon was also harassing her.

The team dismissed the intern a few days later and she retained Minneapolis attorney Lori Peterson to represent her in a sexual harassment in the workplace action.

The intern had known Endy and suspected why he had been dismissed. She told Peterson of her intuitions and the attorney obtained an affidavit from Endy in which he detailed the sexual harassment reports that he had given to Diamond.

Even before the intern filed a lawsuit against the team, the Vikings offered her a settlement of $150,000 in exchange for never discussing the allegations.

Headrick never admitted any wrongdoing on the part of his team, stating that the Vikings had a very "well-defined" policy on sexual harassment and the team would not put up with it.

Criminal behavior in the NFL is an unfortunate byproduct of a society that idolizes its heroes and makes athletes believe they are above the law. Unfortunately for the law-abiding members of the organization—which includes the majority of its players—the Vikings have had more than their share of incidents over the years.

COACH MEATBALL AND HIS SUPER BOWL TICKETS

> Psst. Over here. Yeah, you. Come here. I know you're looking for 'em and I've got 'em. No, I'm legit. I'm not a cop. If you want these tickets it will be $1,900 apiece. You don't want to pay that much? I'm walking.

Mike Tice might not have finished that sale, but he did complete others. That would be fine if he were a car dealer selling new cars. Or a haberdasher selling clothes. But when you are an NFL coach selling Super Bowl tickets at a major profit, that's a major no-no.

Nevertheless, that's just what Mike Tice did prior to Super Bowl XXXIX in Jacksonville. It made Tice and the league the butt of jokes on all talk shows from David Letterman down to *The View*.

But while Tice was not the most successful of Vikings coaches—he succeeded Dennis Green in 2002 and lasted through the 2005 season—he was an upfront guy, for whom his players felt genuine affection.

He might have been loud, he might have been obnoxious, but he said what he thought. Tice came across as a common man. There was nothing elitist about him. He was a hard-nosed former tight end and had the size to go with it.

But too many things happened on his watch for owner Zygi Wilf to keep him on board.

The Minnesota Vikings became an embarrassment on his watch, with a ticket-scalping scandal, the infamous lake cruise, and a Whizzinator somewhere in between.

Mike Tice was head coach during a turbulent time for the Vikings, a period in which even the coach himself got busted (for scalping his Super Bowl tickets).

Nine wins were not enough to keep from getting fired.

Tice did not even have a chance to get some sleep following his final game, a win over the Chicago Bears. Tice went to his office near the Metrodome, where he was joined by Wilf and Wilf's brother Mark, a minority stockholder in the club, who apprised him of their decision not to renew his contract.

His players genuinely liked Tice. Not because he was easy on them, but because he was straightforward—something he was not after he scalped Super Bowl tickets the year before. He didn't come clean until he admitted his misdeed to the league and Red McCombs, the Vikings owner at the time.

"I probably shouldn't have sold my tickets," Tice said. "I made a mistake. I regret it. I'll never do it again. I'm going to be in trouble. I'll probably get slapped with a big fine."

Tice had originally admitted selling tickets while he was an assistant coach but denied doing it after he was named head coach. Tice told NFL security investigators that he scalped part of his allotment of 12 tickets to Super Bowl XXXIX.

"I sold some of my tickets this year," Tice said. "I did. I told the league that and I told [team owner] Red McCombs that. I'm not going to lie. But if I'm going to be thrown out this year for selling tickets, then I'm a scapegoat. If I'm guilty of anything, I'm guilty of selling some of my tickets. I am not guilty of buying any player tickets since I've been made the head coach [in January 2002]."

Tice was not suspended for a year, as he feared. But he was fined a whopping $100,000.

In addition to the Super Bowl ticket fiasco, running back Onterrio Smith was caught at the airport with a device designed to beat drug tests dubbed the "Original Whizzinator." But perhaps the biggest blow came with revelations of an out-of-control boat party during the team's bye week in 2005 that produced misdemeanor charges against four players.

TRIVIA

In what two years as a pro did Leroy Hoard score no touchdowns?

Find the answers on pages 193–194.

Tice's Vikings were inconsistent on the field, prone to long winning streaks and big collapses. Minnesota started 6–0 in 2003 and 5–1 in 2004 before going 3–7 over the final 10 games of both seasons. After starting 2–5 in 2005, the Vikings won six straight, then lost two in a row to fall out of contention for the playoffs.

"After significant evaluation, we feel that now is the time to make a coaching change," Wilf said in the statement.

Tice did not hide his feelings after the decision. "Of course I'm hurt. I'm a man, not a machine," Tice said. "I put a lot of time into this organization, and had a lot of good times, and some bad times."

But the bad taste would not linger. He soon joined former Vikings linebacker and current Jaguars head coach Jack Del Rio in Jacksonville, where he took over as offensive coordinator.

THE TROUBLED ROAD OF RANDY MOSS

The NFL values character. The NFL values citizenship and maintaining a strong public image. These characteristics are far more important than speed, strength, and toughness. Given the choice between a good citizen who is an average player and a guy who has been arrested two or three times but can change a game around in an instant, the league will always go for the Boy Scout.

Yeah, right.

Call it the Neanderthal gene. It's what makes some people career criminals and felons. It makes other people great football players. And it makes some people both.

The Vikings have had their share of players with off-the-field issues. Okay, more than their share. But in order to have a great team, a team has to take a chance every now and then. That's just the position the Vikings found themselves in when they drafted Randy Moss in 1998. Moss was clearly the best receiver in his draft class after a stellar career at Marshall. Never mind the mid-major label, Moss's skill levels were off the charts. He was able to dominate games with his size, strength, speed, leaping ability, and hands.

Scouts were simply drooling over his ability to change the direction of any game. Talk about an impact player, that was Moss.

But he had just a little bit of baggage. In 1995, he pleaded guilty to two counts of battery for kicking another student during his senior year of high school in Rand, West Virginia. He was sentenced to 30 days in prison.

As a freshman at Florida State, Moss tested positive for marijuana. He was also involved in a domestic dispute with his girlfriend. Charges were later dropped.

Those issues and a defiant, aggressive attitude scared off a lot of teams in the NFL. On draft day in 1998, he did not go with the first, second, or third pick to the Colts, Chargers, or Cardinals. Those picks were Peyton Manning (no argument), Ryan Leaf (one of the worst picks of all-time), and Andre Wadsworth (stand up if you remember this underachieving defensive end from Florida State).

The Raiders took Michigan star cornerback Charles Woodson with the fourth pick and the Bears made the regrettable decision to draft Curtis Enis with the fifth pick.

Moss was clearly in a freefall after the Raiders and Bears passed on him. As the teams continued to pass on Moss as the first hours went by in the draft. The Vikings, with the number 21 pick in the draft, didn't believe they would have a shot at drafting him. Even if some teams were afraid of his background, he would clearly go in the top 10.

No, he didn't. When the Patriots drafted Georgia running back Robert Edwards with the 18th pick, head coach Dennis Green began to think the Vikings had a chance. He didn't dare dream of pairing Moss with All-Pro Cris Carter because the Packers and Lions still had a chance to make their picks. But that's exactly how it fell when Green's division rivals both passed on the stud.

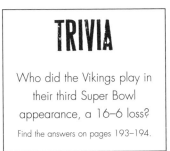

TRIVIA

Who did the Vikings play in their third Super Bowl appearance, a 16–6 loss?

Find the answers on pages 193–194.

Green might have had several flaws as a head coach, but he has shown he can work with myriad quarterbacks and give them a slew of weapons to work with. He also demonstrated he could take "difficult" players and build their self-esteem and make them feel welcome.

Moss did not need the Welcome Wagon routine. He had more than enough motivation because of the way he had been snubbed in the draft. He was particularly upset that the Dallas Cowboys had passed on him. "I was stuck on Dallas and I really wanted to play there," Moss said. "It wasn't even funny."

Green knew he had something special at the start of training camp and Moss was not about to come into the league on his tip toes. Instead, he came out charging, determined to make each and every one of the 20 teams that picked before the Vikings regret their selection.

He was also playing at what he considered a bargain price. To be conservative, if Moss had been a top 10 choice, he would have received a contract in the $6 million range under the NFL's slotting system. As the number 21 pick, Moss signed a contract that paid him $1.4 million in his first season. He took out his anger on the rest of the league.

Moss caught two touchdown passes from quarterback Brad Johnson against the Tampa Bay Bucs in the season opener before the game had reached halftime. Moss continued to play with drive and intensity every week, and it was apparent the Vikings had found themselves a star with their first-round pick.

They were also dominating the league. Even though Johnson went down with a broken leg in the second week of the season against the Rams, the Vikings didn't miss a beat as veteran Randall Cunningham replaced him seamlessly. Many scouts around the league actually thought that Cunningham was the better quarterback for the Vikings because he had a stronger arm that would allow him to take advantage of Moss's ability to make plays downfield.

As the wins kept mounting up, so did Moss's touchdown receptions. He became the focal point of the Vikings offense, catching 17 touchdown passes in his rookie year. That absurd total led longtime NFL scouts to scratch their heads and say that they knew he was a great player but that they'd had no idea he'd be able to play like that as a rookie. "I knew he had once-in-a-lifetime ability," said one AFC general manager. "But who knew he could put it all together in his first year. He was truly amazing that year—outperforming all the best stars at his position including Mr. Rice."

Mr. Rice, of course, was Jerry Rice of the 49ers. Almost unanimously considered the best player at his position to ever play the game, Rice owns nearly all of the NFL's significant receiving records. But in addition to his all-around talent, Rice always was one of the hardest-working players in the league. He would put himself through a very demanding off-season regimen in order to be in tip-top shape by the time training camp began. He didn't do that once, he did it every year.

Carter, who had taken Moss under his wing from the moment he was drafted, knew that his young teammate had all the ability and talent that a wide receiver could possibly have. But having been through his own travails in his career, he knew that Moss had quite a bit of work to do in order to be consistently great.

Moss was very appreciative of the role Carter played in the early part of his career. "He plays the biggest role of anyone," Moss said. "I play off him. Cris is the main guy."

That was on the practice field and during games. Once his responsibilities on the field were done, they each went their separate ways. Not because they didn't like each other, but they were

Randy Moss ignores reporters as he waits for his ride after his release from jail on September 25, 2002. Moss was arrested and charged with two misdemeanors after an incident involving a female traffic director.

MOSS SHOVES TRAFFIC OFFICER

Of all the incidents that made headlines during Randy Moss's tenure with the Vikings, the worst was no doubt the time he used his car to push a traffic agent for having the temerity to keep him from making an illegal turn in 2002.

Moss spent a night in jail after the 27-year-old agent stepped in front of Moss to stop him from making an illegal turn in downtown Minneapolis, and Moss used his 2002 Lexus to slowly push the officer a half-block along the street, stopping when she fell to the ground, police spokeswoman Cyndi Barrington said.

Amy Zaccardi, a city employee but not a police officer, was not seriously hurt. Witnesses called the situation "surreal" but said it was clear Moss did not intend to hurt Zaccardi.

Moss flatly "denied doing what the police said that he did."

Minneapolis resident Jerry Hullerman said he saw the incident while parked near the intersection.

"I saw a really decked-out Lexus pushing the traffic person along," said Hullerman, who was also interviewed by police. "It was really surreal."

He said the agent was facing forward while sitting on the front of the car with one hand on the hood and the other hand on her radio as the car pushed her along.

After a few seconds, Hullerman said, the man in the car tapped the accelerator and knocked her down. "She fell flat on her face," Hullerman said, adding that the driver didn't get out of his car.

Hullerman said squad cars arrived seconds later and officers took Moss into custody.

Other witnesses confirmed Hullerman's story.

Moss later apologized to his teammates, coaches, and family. He did not apologize to Zaccardi.

Head coach Mike Tice stuck up for Moss at the time, saying he had been "an asset to the community," but Minnesota was not buying it. After that incident, Vikings fans tolerated Moss, but once his production went down he had to go. He could not rehabilitate his image and a relationship between a team and a player that started so well ended in shame.

just at different stages in life. Carter was married with a family and wanted only to stay away from demons like alcohol and cocaine that had almost ruined his life. Moss was young and loved to party.

Carter never believed that awards, honors, and pats on the back were necessary for players to win respect in the locker room. But he was hoping that Moss would win a spot in the Pro Bowl in his rookie year. He knew that if Moss got a look at the way Rice prepared for a meaningless game like the Pro Bowl, it might make an impression on him. Rice never looked at the week in Hawaii as a reward for a job well done during the year. It was one more opportunity to work on his skills and push himself to get better.

Other players in the league were awed and amazed by Rice's attention to detail and capacity to push himself.

Carter wasn't the only one who thought Moss had the potential to have a career that was similar to Rice's. After seeing Moss catch three more touchdown passes than any other receiver in the league and finished his rookie season with 69 receptions for 1,313 yards and 17 scores, Vikings offensive coordinator Brian Billick (who would later win a Super Bowl as head coach of the Ravens) thought Moss had more talent to work with than any receiver in league history.

"I don't think it's out of line to say that Randy has the potential to be the greatest receiver ever," Billick said. "It's in his hands to get the most out of himself. In order to do that, it will take a monumental amount of work."

Nobody ever expected Moss to rival Rice, but if he could be a bit more dedicated, Vikings coaches were hopeful that the big brother attitude of Carter and the sight of Rice working like a demon in Hawaii would make a major impression on Moss.

It didn't. Moss still had his brilliant all-around talent and that was good enough for him. When it came to doing the extra things to get better, Moss was more interested in enjoying himself and doing things at his own pace. His lack of devotion to his craft didn't show up in the numbers, but his attitude reflected a certain contempt for authority that would result in obnoxious incidents over the years.

Moss continued to play like a driven man in the ensuing years. He caught 80 passes for 1,413 yards and 11 touchdowns in his second year with the Vikings and caught 77 passes for 1,437 yards and 15 touchdowns in 2000. He was an unstoppable force, but there was also a troubling pattern of incidents that included squirting a water bottle at an official in a loss at Kansas City and frequent gestures toward quarterback Daunte Culpepper when he thought the quarterback missed him when he was open.

But there was another problem developing with Moss's game. At first it showed up in road games against super-aggressive defenses, but then it popped up on the road and finally at home.

TRIVIA

Who is the Vikings' all-time leader in blocked kicks, and how many does he have?

Find the answers on pages 193–194.

Moss developed a case of alligator arms, a disease that can be fatal for a wideout.

On an athlete as dominating as Moss, the problem was devastating to his reputation. He continued to put up huge numbers—reaching a career-high 111 catches for 1,632 yards with 17 touchdowns in 2003—but his reluctance to catch the short- and medium-range pass over the middle was a major issue. The contrast between his effort on those passes and the jump ball in the end zone over a 5'10" cornerback was startling. The problem with a player who possesses maximum ability and chooses not to use it at all times is that he's not fooling anybody—especially his teammates and coaches.

Over the years, he also showed he was an inconsistent blocker and didn't always run his routes precisely when he wasn't the main focus of the offense. In short, he had many childish characteristics that shouted "I'm going to take my ball and go home if you don't throw it to me when and where I want it."

In his last year with the Vikings, Moss's lack of effort was particularly appalling against the Chicago Bears. Covered by rookie defensive back Charles Tillman in Week 13 of the 2004 season, Culpepper threw Moss what looked like a sure touchdown pass on a short pass in the red zone. Just as Moss got his hands on the ball,

MOSS FINES IN MINNESOTA

- January 2005: $10,000 for "Moon over Green Bay"
- November 2001: $15,000 for yelling at sponsors on bus
- November 2001: $10,000 for taunting New York Giants
- November 2000: $25,000 for touching an official
- January 2000: $25,000 for squirting official with water
- November 1999: $10,000 for yelling at official

Tillman stepped in and stole it away from him. In the process of bringing the ball into his body, Tillman overpowered Moss and showed far more fire than the receiver. After an instant of stunned silence, the Soldier Field crowd erupted in a cacophony of noise. Not only was it a stunning play, it also helped the lowly Bears pull off a 24–14 victory over the playoff-bound Vikings.

In the postseason, Moss wanted to demonstrate he was still a great player even though his reception total had fallen to 49 catches for 767 yards and 13 touchdowns in 13 games. Minnesota was an underdog in its wild-card game against the Packers. However, Culpepper was hot and the Vikings pulled off a 31–17 upset. After catching a touchdown pass from Culpepper, Moss decided to show the Green Bay crowd what he thought of them after hearing their taunts.

In an era when wide receivers were drawing attention to themselves with touchdown celebrations like pulling out a Sharpie and autographing the ball (Terrell Owens) or taking a cell phone out of a sock and calling a friend (Joe Horn), Moss pantomimed that he was wiping his butt on the goalpost. It was a childish and sickening act that was labeled as such by Fox national broadcaster Joe Buck.

Moss wore out his welcome with the Vikings and was traded to Oakland for a first-round choice, a seventh-round choice, and linebacker Napoleon Harris in 2005. Moss played ineffectively on a poor team and has done nothing to resuscitate his reputation.

TRADING PLACES

THE VIKINGS GREW FROM BOTH TARKENTON TRADES

The Vikings have a significant history when it comes to making blockbuster trades.

Two stand out more than any of the others. One of them helped turn a good young team into a great one; the other sent the team into a tailspin and would be recognized as one of the worst trades in NFL history.

Fran Tarkenton had been the face of the Vikings franchise since the team came into the league in 1961. He was clearly a brilliant athlete who could fire the rock as well as any of the bigger quarterbacks in the league and could move faster than any of his contemporaries. His ability to run the ball made for some spectacular highlights, but it was his arm strength, accuracy, and guts that gave the Vikings a chance to win.

While a quarterback who can move is almost a "must have" in today's NFL, a quarterback who would not sit back in the pocket and survey the field before throwing was viewed as a weakness in the 1960s—at least it was by some, and none more than Head Coach Norm Van Brocklin. A Hall of Fame quarterback who played for the Rams and Eagles, Van Brocklin obviously understood the nuances of the position.

Van Brocklin should also be in the Hall of Fame for arrogance and stubbornness. It was his way or else, and Tarkenton's way often irritated him to no end. While Fran was his quarterback for the team's first six years, the relationship was anything but smooth. Van Brocklin didn't have full respect for Tarkenton's game and Fran knew it. Tarkenton was able to bear up under the circumstances but resented Van Brocklin's lack of appreciation.

Tarkenton's prayers appeared to be answered in February 1967 when the old Dutchman resigned. Van Brocklin would later become the head coach of the Falcons—and his departure from Minnesota would be viewed as good news for all the Vikings players who were tired of hearing their coach turn up the volume and let them know how awful they were.

Van Brocklin's style was not a lot different from many of the head coaches of the time, but few had

TRIVIA

Who holds the record for most opponents' fumbles recovered in a game?
Find the answers on pages 193–194.

the ability to get under their players' skin the way he could. Van Brocklin clearly had a mean streak and a lack of patience.

While many of the Vikings players were celebrating as they wondered who their next coach would be, the team decided to trade Tarkenton, their strongest asset. It was a move that few would understand at the time, but one that would pay huge dividends in the years to come.

Tarkenton was traded to the New York Giants on March 7, 1967, for a first- and second-round draft choice in 1967, a first-round choice in '68, and a second-round choice in '69. Important pieces of their soon-to-be dominant teams would come in the draft choices they received from the Giants. They selected running back Clint Jones and wide receiver Bob Grim in '67, offensive tackle Ron Yary in '68, and guard Ed White in '69.

Yary and White would become Vikings offensive line fixtures. Yary is widely recognized as one of the top offensive linemen in the league's history and was inducted into the Hall of Fame in 2001. Jones and Grim were both solid players, but not quite superstars.

Tarkenton would go on to play very respectably for a putrid Giants team. They were among the least talented teams in the league and at times Sir Francis was their only player who could actually make things happen.

The trade was a huge victory for the Vikings. They changed the image of their team with the move. While Van Brocklin was gone, his belief that a scrambling quarterback was bad for the football team had permeated the organization. The Vikings got maximum return for their superstar and also made themselves younger in the process.

The trade preceded the hiring of Canadian Football League coach Bud Grant to take over for Van Brocklin. General manager Jim Finks had tremendous respect for Grant's quiet intensity and outstanding coaching attributes.

Van Brocklin and Grant were polar opposites in personality. Grant had quiet, athletic confidence and a sharp blue-eyed stare that could weaken the knees of the toughest men. He also treated his players like men; something that could never be said of Van Brocklin.

After Grant was on board, the Vikings would bring in CFL veteran Joe Kapp to take over at quarterback. While not as stylish as Tarkenton, Kapp got the job done with guts, determination, and pride.

There were no immediate dividends as the Vikings went 3–8–3 in '67, but they would go 8–6 the next year and make the playoffs for the first time. It would start an era in which the Vikings would become not only one of the best teams in the league but also the classiest. While Van Brocklin had been a belligerent dictator, Grant was known for his dignity and intelligence.

WALKER DEAL A COSTLY STINKER

The Vikings would make headlines with another trade 22 years later. GM Mike Lynn thought his team had a chance to get to the Super Bowl in 1989 after losing to the 49ers in the divisional play-offs the year before. After watching his team struggle in the running game with the likes of Rick Fenney, D.J. Dozier, and Alfred Anderson carrying the ball, Lynn decided he had to upgrade the running game.

The Vikings' trade for Herschel Walker from the Dallas Cowboys has gone down as one of the most lopsided in NFL history.

He looked to Dallas and its super stud Herschel Walker. An elite athlete and a top-level performer, Walker could clearly give the Vikings a lift at the position after rushing for 1,514 yards in 1988. He was averaging just 3.0 yards per carry through the early part of the season, but Lynn wasn't worried. He should have been.

TRIVIA

Who holds the Vikings record for interceptions in a season?

Find the answers on pages 193–194.

Walker would run for 669 yards in 11 games with the Vikings—hardly the kind of totals that Lynn or head coach Jerry Burns had anticipated. The following year wasn't much better as Walker ran for 770 yards and five touchdowns.

But Walker was not really the problem. He might not have reached expectations, but he was still a productive player who improved the Minnesota running game. The problem was Lynn, who got hornswoggled in the trade by Dallas head coach Jimmy Johnson.

Johnson, a rookie coach at the time, had a team with very little talent. They were going to lose with Walker or without him, so he decided to maximize his top asset by trading him.

The Cowboys received five players and eight draft picks in exchange for Walker and four draft picks. Johnson was able to turn the Cowboys into a championship team with the players and draft picks while the Vikings would backslide and become an ordinary team. The trade established Johnson as one of the shrewdest wheeler-dealers in the league and it demonstrated that Lynn had no business running a pro football team. He became a target for the fans' anger when the trade did not work out. Lynn, distant and cold, became one of the most disliked figures in Minnesota sports history.

He would eventually be forced out of his position, but it was too little and too late for Vikings fans—who wished he had been let out of his position before he encountered a horse trader from Texas named Johnson.

Walker said his involvement in the trade is the biggest regret of his sporting career. "I knew it was never going to work from the start," Walker said. "I feel bad about that. It wasn't my fault, but I feel I cheated Minnesota because I don't think the people there ever really saw me play.

"I remember a slogan from this TV show and this guy looked at his sergeant and said, 'we can't do much with these broomsticks.' They were not letting them fight in the war. They were letting them sweep the floor. I was sort of in the same situation. I couldn't do too much on the sideline. They weren't letting me play. I loved Minneapolis and I loved the people there. They treated me well. There was just so much more that I could do for them than what I did."

TARKENTON RETURNS

Fran Tarkenton had left the Vikings under the worst of circumstances. He had been berated and belittled by a coach who did not appreciate his array of talent. The trade to the Giants was good for him because it gave him a fresh start and got him out of an environment that had become oppressive.

Tarkenton produced consistently in New York and the Giants were competitive throughout his tenure there in all but one season. They nearly made the playoffs in 1970, needing a win in the season finale against the Los Angeles Rams to have that opportunity. While the Rams were a strong team led by Deacon Jones, Merlin Olsen, Roman Gabriel, and Jack Snow, the Giants jumped out to a 3–0 lead.

The early lead was merely a blip on the radar screen and the Rams ended the Giants season with a 31–3 defeat.

It was clear the Giants were a long way from the Super Bowl and Tarkenton wanted an opportunity to get there. He wanted to get traded and the Vikings were interested. They had finished with an 11–3 record in 1971 with Gary Cuozzo, Bob Lee, and Norm Snead dividing the quarterback chores. Production from that trio was a major problem. The Vikings quarterbacks completed 47 percent of their passes and they threw only nine touchdown passes while handing out 18 interceptions.

Minnesota met Dallas in the first round of the playoffs and suffered a 20–12 home loss to Roger Staubach's team. It was obvious to Finks that the Vikings needed to upgrade.

AN UGLY DIVORCE: CULPEPPER TRADED TO MIAMI

He was the quarterback with the golden gun, the great wheels, and unlimited potential.

When the Vikings drafted Daunte Culpepper with the 11th overall pick in 1999, most fans were scratching their heads. They knew Culpepper was a huge man (6'4", 264 pounds) from a relatively unknown school (Central Florida) with supposedly unlimited potential.

All that was nice, but nobody knew what Culpepper could do when jumping to the next level.

Head coach Denny Green did not force Culpepper into action during his rookie season. He got a chance to watch two veteran quarterbacks up close and personal as Randall Cunningham and Jeff George handled the quarterbacking duties for the 10–6 Vikings.

But Green knew he had a big-time stud at quarterback and he didn't want to wait any longer to insert Culpepper into the lineup. Green did not bring Jeff George back for the 2000 season and turned the quarterbacking responsibilities over to Culpepper.

The quarterback had an explosive debut, leading the Vikings to a season-opening 30–27 win over the Chicago Bears. Culpepper had just an average day passing—completing 13 of 23 passes for 193 yards—but he was nearly unstoppable running the football. He carried 13 times for 73 yards and three touchdowns.

To longtime Vikings fans, Culpepper was a giant-sized version of Hall of Famer Fran Tarkenton.

Culpepper went on to perform spectacularly during his first season as a starter, throwing 33 touchdown passes for 3,937 yards. He also ran for 470 yards and appeared to be a weapon of destruction for the Vikings offense. The Vikings won the NFC Central division, defeated the Saints 34–16 in the divisional playoffs, and earned a spot in the NFC championship game against the Giants.

Could the Vikings go into the Meadowlands and get the best of Jim Fassel's Giants with a rookie quarterback at the controls? The feeling around the team was that if the Falcons were able to go into the Metrodome and beat the 15–1 Vikings two years earlier, there was no reason the Vikings couldn't go on the road and beat a 12–4 Giants team—even with a rookie quarterback.

Reality turned out to be quite different from theory. The Vikings were overwhelmed from the start, getting bombed 41–0.

That loss didn't take the sheen off of Culpepper's achievements, but it planted a seed of doubt in his mind.

The 2001 season was not as easy as Culpepper's physical play began to take a toll. He struggled with consistency and threw 14 touchdowns and 13 interceptions before he was finished for the season in early December.

Culpepper was inconsistent again in 2002. He often had a hard time reading defenses and often tried to force passes into coverage. While Green never lost faith in him, wideouts Cris Carter and Randy Moss could be seen regularly getting in Culpepper's face. While the three of them all got along well, it created the impression that the receivers did not respect the quarterback.

Culpepper bounced back with magnificent seasons in 2003 and 2004. The '04 season was beyond what anyone could have hoped for as Culpepper completed 69.2 percent of his passes for 4,717 yards with 39 touchdowns and 11 interceptions. He also ran for 406 yards and two touchdowns.

Culpepper might have been off the charts, but he was eclipsed by Peyton Manning, who threw an NFL-record 49 touchdown passes for the Colts. Vikings fans didn't care. Their huge quarterback had put two excellent seasons back-to-back and was surely over his problems of inconsistency.

However, when Culpepper came to training camp in 2005, he no longer had Moss at his disposal. The controversial playmaker had been traded to the Raiders and Culpepper looked lost without him.

Culpepper got off to a miserable start in 2005, forcing the ball into coverage and throwing 12 interceptions with just six touchdowns. The Vikings were 2–4 heading into a game at Carolina against the physical Panthers. Disaster struck when Culpepper suffered a major knee injury that forced him onto injured reserve.

Culpepper had been involved in the infamous "Love Boat" scandal a few weeks before the injury, and his involvement completely changed his image with the team. The combination of the injury and the incident led Vikings management to the conclusion that Culpepper's best days with the team were behind him.

At the end of the 2005 season, the Vikings fired head coach Mike Tice and brought in Brad Childress. The new coach was not thrilled with the idea of the rehabbing Culpepper coming back to the Vikings in 2006. Culpepper was hurt by the rumblings and asked for a trade.

The divorce between Culpepper and the team was finalized March 15, 2006, when he was traded to the Dolphins for a second-round draft pick. The Vikings used that pick to select center Ryan Cook from New Mexico. Cook played in six games as a rookie, starting three of them.

Culpepper for Cook?

Although Culpepper was unable to complete his first season in Miami as he never fully recovered from his 2005 knee injury, it seems like the Vikings didn't get anywhere near the value they could have for their record-setting quarterback.

As Brad Johnson, Brooks Bollinger, and rookie Tavaris Jackson stumbled and bumbled at the position during 2006, Vikings fans were not happy with the team's quarterback prospects for the future.

Those doubts have plenty of merit.

The idea of bringing Tarkenton back was more than logical. Not only did Vikings fans remember everything he had done in the early years of the franchise, they also knew he was far better than any quarterback on the Minnesota roster. He would make the Vikings a competitive offensive team and the team seemed to have endless possibilities if it could put together a productive offense to go with that destructive defense.

Finks pulled the trigger on the trade. He reacquired Tarkenton in exchange for wide receiver Bob Grim, running back Vince Clements, and Norm Snead along with a first-round draft choice in 1972 and a third-rounder in '73. It was a high price to pay, but Finks and Bud Grant thought that it just might make the Vikings a Super Bowl team.

Tarkenton had a strong season while getting re-acclimated in '72, but the Vikings were just a 7–7 team. The next season, Minnesota clicked on all cylinders and went 12–2 in the regular season. Minnesota played overpowering and intimidating football in beating the Redskins and Cowboys to win the NFC and gain a spot in the Super Bowl. Unfortunately for Minnesota, the Vikings had to go up against the substantial presence of Don Shula's Dolphins. Miami dominated behind Bob Griese and a great offensive line during a 24–7 victory.

TRIVIA

Who holds the Vikings record for consecutive rushing attempts without a fumble?

Find the answers on pages 193–194.

Tarkenton would play in two more Super Bowls and play through the 1978 season. By that time, he was widely recognized as one of the best quarterbacks in the history of the game. He never won a Super Bowl, but he gave the Vikings a chance to play as well on the offensive end as they did on defense.

Reacquiring him in 1972 turned out to be one of the best moves the team ever made.

WANNA BET?

A FOOL AND HIS MONEY...

Do you see the Vikings fan in the Helga Hat sitting at the bar with his head in his hands? Everyone else around him is celebrating and raising a drink because the Vikings have just won.

But why is our friend at the bar so distraught? Because the Vikings have failed to cover the spread yet again. Gambling is among the biggest reasons the NFL has reached its tremendous heights, and while the league "officially" wants to divorce itself from point-spread wagering on its product, it is an undeniable fact of life.

Those who gamble on games know that betting can result in a win for their team yet a painful defeat in the pocketbook if their team is favored and fails to win by enough points.

Over the years, Vikings backers have endured more than their share of painful defeats where the spread is concerned. The "meaningless" touchdown in the final minute of the game or the failure to score when running out the clock has caused more angst for Vikings backers than nearly any other team in the league. Not the kind of defeat that hurts for a day, but one that awakens the bettor in the middle of the night in a cold sweat.

Following are some of the more painful defeats that Vikings supporters have suffered throughout the years.

1. Vikings 31, Cardinals 26, Metrodome, November 26, 2006—The Vikings had gotten off to a 4–2 start in Brad Childress's

A Vikings fan covers his face with his Helga Hat after the Green Bay Packers kicked a 29-yard field goal with three seconds left in the game to beat the Vikings 34–31 on December 24, 2004.

first year as head coach, but the promise slipped away with four straight losses. When former head coach Dennis Green brought his struggling Arizona Cardinals to the Metrodome, the Vikings had a chance to get well.

Las Vegas oddsmakers had installed the Vikings as 6.5-point favorites and the Vikings offense was ripping through the Cardinals defense. The Vikings had built a 31–13 lead with 12 minutes to go in the fourth quarter when Brad Johnson hit Jeff Dugan with a 4-yard touchdown pass.

The Vikings were about to add to their lead when they had the ball deep in Arizona territory less than two minutes later, and Johnson handed the ball off to running back Chester Taylor at the

1-yard line. Instead of plowing into the end zone, Taylor fumbled the ball and Cardinals safety Adrian Wilson picked it up and ran 99 yards for an Arizona touchdown.

That play was a shocker, but the Vikings seemed to have the spread covered along with the win...until Cardinals quarterback Matt Leinart hit wideout Anquan Boldin with a 9-yard touchdown pass with only 39 seconds left on the clock. Vikings fans were grateful to escape with a 31–26 win, but those who had bet on the Vikings were beside themselves. Their easy cover turned out to be a day of agony.

2. **Dolphins 24, Vikings 20, Dolphin Stadium, November 19, 2006**—The week before the Cardinals debacle, the Vikings stole

Whether it be amidst the backdrop of the sports book at Caeser's Palace Casino or back home in Minnesota, Vikings fans have endured suffering in their hearts—and their wallets. The team has been notorious for failing to cover point spreads.

defeat from the jaws of victory. Minnesota played Miami extremely well into the fourth quarter, leading 13–10 with fewer than 10 minutes remaining in the fourth quarter as a three-point underdog.

TRIVIA

Who is second to Fran Tarkenton on the career touchdown pass list?

Find the answers on pages 193–194.

The Vikings had the ball near midfield and were driving. However, Taylor got hammered in the backfield for a two-yard loss and he dropped the football after a hit by the Dolphins' Matt Roth. Cornerback Renaldo Hill picked up the ball and returned it 48 yards for a touchdown. Dolphins led 17–13. The Dolphins added another defensive score when Jason Taylor picked off a Johnson pass and returned it 51 yards for a touchdown.

The Vikings made it close when Taylor scored on a one-yard run with no time remaining on the clock, but that touchdown left the Vikings with yet another defeat against the spread. The one-point loss against the spread was a narrow margin, but they don't pay off in Vegas for keeping it close.

3. **Vikings 27, Bears 22, Metrodome, September 26, 2004—** The Vikings were 11.5-point favorites against a Bears team trying to find an identity under first-year head coach Lovie Smith with inexperienced Rex Grossman at quarterback. The Vikings had a 17–6 lead at the end of the third quarter and appeared to have the cover when Daunte Culpepper threw a two-yard touchdown pass to Randy Moss with just 5:39 left in the game. However, Grossman led the Bears on a late drive and scored on a five-yard run with two minutes to go that got the Bears inside the magic number. Grossman paid a price for the touchdown, however, as he tore up his knee on his final step into the end zone.

4. **Vikings 24, Lions 14, Metrodome, November 23, 2003—** Minnesota backers were glum as the fourth quarter started. The Vikings led 10–7 and as 10.5-point favorites it appeared that there was no way their listless team would cover against woeful Detroit. However, with 2:26 remaining in the fourth quarter, Corey Chavous intercepted a Joey Harrington pass and returned it 32

yards for a touchdown. The Vikings were now close to covering at 17–7, but there was little time remaining on the clock. Clearly it would take another defensive touchdown to give them the cover. While that appeared too much to hope for, Brian Williams picked

TRIVIA

Which three Vikings share the record for rushing yards in a game?

Find the answers on pages 193–194.

off the generous Harrington 20 seconds later and went 42 yards for the score. Jubilation in the stands! Dancing in the aisles! The Vikings had a 24–7 lead at the two-minute warning and the shell-shocked Harrington was still at quarterback. While fans were wiping away their tears of happiness and counting their money, Harrington led the

Lions on a last-minute drive and shocked the Vikings backers with a five-yard touchdown pass to Az-Zahir Hakim with 35 seconds left. Agony had befallen Vikings backers once again.

5. Vikings 23, Rams 21 (OT), Metrodome, November 5, 1989—This might have been the mother of all spread losses. The Vikings were 4.5-point favorites over the Rams, which seemed like a major bargain because Minnesota had won its first four home games by an average of 16 points a game. Additionally, the Rams had lost their previous two road games and it didn't look as if they would be able to stay on the field with the Vikings. Minnesota's defense held up its end of the bargain, holding the Rams to one touchdown as the game reached the fourth quarter. The Vikings offense did a great job of moving the football, but could not punch it in. Head coach Jerry Burns seethed on the sidelines as his team settled for field goals. Barefooted Rich Karlis kicked six of them and five were less than 30 yards. Still, the Vikings had an 18–7 lead as the game reached its late stages.

The Rams dented the Vikings' spirits when quarterback Jim Everett hit Henry Ellard with a six-yard touchdown pass to make it 18–14 and the Rams took the lead on a one-yard touchdown run from Greg Bell. With the Rams leading 21–18, Karlis came to the rescue by hitting a 40-yard field goal to force overtime.

Given another life, the Vikings defense showed its muscle and forced a Ram three-and-out in the extra session. Speedy linebacker Mike Merriweather broke through the protection and blocked Dale Hatcher's punt deep in Rams territory. The ball bounded back into the end zone and Merriweather raced back to fall on it for a winning touchdown that would have given the Vikings the cover. Instead, the ball somehow squirted away from Merriweather and headed to the back line. The Vikings had two more chances to recover the ball in the end zone, but they were never able to secure it. The ball ended up going through the end zone and the resulting safety gave Minnesota the win but gave the Rams the cover. That was the first time in the history of the NFL that a safety had ended an overtime game and it has only happened one other time since then.

Combine the squirming finish with the missed opportunities early on and it's clearly one of the most painful defeats in the history of sports gambling.

A LITTLE PAYBACK

It hasn't been all bad news for Vikings supporters. While the defeats are far more memorable than the victories, there have been some wins that have to be classified as incredible.

During the 2006 season, the Vikings hosted the Carolina Panthers in Week 2. Minnesota had won its opener at Washington and rookie head coach Brad Childress had some momentum as they came home to face the team that many considered the favorite to represent the NFC in the Super Bowl.

The Vikings were unimpressed and were installed as two-point favorites. Both teams played a physical, punishing game and the Panthers held a 13–6 lead midway through the fourth quarter. Place-kicker Ryan Longwell lined up to attempt a 33-yard field goal that would have brought the Vikings within four points. But Childress wanted to surprise the Panthers and Longwell did not attempt the kick. Instead, he took a pitchout from holder Chris Kluwe and rolled to his right. Longwell shocked the Panthers by throwing a 16-yard touchdown pass to tight end Richard Owens

TRIVIA

Who holds the Vikings
record for receiving yards
in a game?

Find the answers on pages 193–194.

that tied the score. The Vikings then got the win and the cover when Longwell hit a 19-yard field goal in the extra session.

In the magical 15–1 season in 1998, the Vikings were nearly as dominant against the number as they were on the scoreboard. Prior to their heart-wrenching loss to the Falcons in the NFC championship game, the Vikings were 7–0–1 in their previous eight games against the spread.

The most memorable of those games was their 46–36 Thanksgiving Day victory over the Cowboys in Dallas. In that game, the Vikings flexed their offensive muscles by scoring early and often as a three-point favorite against a Dallas defense that was just overmatched. Randy Moss, in the midst of a 17-touchdown season as a rookie, caught three touchdown passes, all of which were for 50 yards or more. While the Cowboys were able to get their share of points, the outcome was never in doubt and Thanksgiving dinner never tasted as good as it did on that day.

UP AND DOWN

PUNCHING BAGS: THE VIKINGS HANDLED THE RAMS AND THE LIONS WITH EASE

The Vikings have clearly had their problems in the Super Bowl, with significant losses to the Chiefs, Dolphins, Steelers, and Raiders, in that order. Bud Grant's team—no matter how dominant in the regular season and playoff games—just could not produce on the biggest stage.

Whether that was because of their opponents' strengths or their own inability to play their best game when they needed it most is up for debate.

But the Vikings have had their share of patsies as well. Most notable was their domination of the Rams at home through their 1976 playoff game. Minnesota won 10 of 13 home games against the Rams (two ended in ties), including three playoff games that left their opponents talking to themselves. The Rams felt they had outplayed their hosts in several of the games, but they just couldn't take advantage of them on the scoreboard.

During the regular season, the Vikings simply owned the Lions from 1968 through 1989. During a 22-year run of domination, the Vikings recorded a 34–8 record against their older rivals, which included 13 straight wins between 1968 and 1974 and a seven-game streak between 1986 and 1989.

Detroit swept the first two season series from the Vikings in 1961 and '62 and did not accomplish the feat again until 1991. They haven't done it since 1997 and the Vikings once again

171

established their dominance by winning 10 games in a row against Detroit through the end of the 2006 season.

Their dominance over the Rams was more memorable because it came in the postseason.

The 1976 NFC championship game between the Rams and Vikings at the Met demonstrated Minnesota's resourcefulness and their opponents' inability to make a big play at the key moment.

The first half ended with the Vikings leading 10–0, even though they had less than 90 yards of total offense. The Vikings special teams were responsible for both scores. They had blocked a punt that led to a Fred Cox field goal, Nate Allen blocked a Tom Dempsey field goal attempt, and the opportunistic Bobby Bryant scooped up the ball and raced 90 yards for a touchdown.

The Dempsey field-goal attempt came after the Rams thought they had gotten into the end zone on two occasions. The first was a reverse by receiver Ron Jessie on second-and-goal from the 4-yard line. Just as Jessie was about to step over the goal line he was pushed out of bounds. Jessie thought he had gotten in and that the officials gave him a bad spot.

Unable to move it on the next play, the Rams head coach sent Dempsey in to attempt a 17-yard field goal—closer than an extra point. While it appeared to be the easiest kick possible, Allen was conceding nothing.

"I thought I could block every kick there was," Allen said. "The Vikings were the best in football at blocking kicks. We got 15 of them that year and I got three myself."

The snap from center was a tad wobbly and it took a bit longer than usual to set the ball in place. That was all Allen needed. He blocked the kick and it bounced toward the sidelines. Bryant picked it up on the hop and took it the distance.

On their next possession, the Rams were undeterred and marched to the Vikings' 21. But running back John Cappelletti fumbled on a sweep and speedy linebacker Matt Blair recovered for the Vikings.

Fran Tarkenton was unable to move for the Vikings and seemed more bothered by the 12-degree weather than his counterparts from southern California. Minnesota went three-and-out and punted it back to the Rams. This time they were unable to move and called on Rusty Jackson to punt it away. Jackson dropped the snap, picked it up, and tried to kick it. Blair blocked the kick and the Vikings had it at the 8. Cox converted a 25-yard field goal.

TRIVIA

Who holds the Vikings record for most rushing attempts in a game?

Find the answers on pages 193–194.

The Vikings took that 10–0 lead into halftime and on the second play of the second half, versatile running back Chuck Foreman took advantage of a great block by center Mick Tinglehoff and ran 62 yards up the middle. Tackled at the 2 by Rod Perry, Foreman scored two plays later.

The game appeared to be a rout in the making as Tarkenton finally got acclimated and moved the Vikings down the field to the Rams' 20 through the air. But instead of making it 24–0, Tarkenton was picked off by Monte Jackson. Los Angeles took advantage of the turnover. Quarterback Pat Haden hit Harold Jackson with a 40-yard pass that set up running back Lawrence McCutcheon for a 10-yard touchdown run. While Dempsey missed the extra point, the Rams knew they had all the momentum.

The Rams started to gain confidence and felt even better when Jack Youngblood picked up a Tarkenton fumble and brought it to the Vikings' 8. Haden hit Jackson for a touchdown three plays later.

"I was sure we were going to win," said Youngblood. "We were making big plays. We were making the kind of plays that get you to the Super Bowl."

The Rams got to the Vikings' 33 on their next possession but savvy linebacker Wally Hilgenberg sacked Haden to end the threat and Bryant snuffed out another drive when he intercepted a pass intended for Jessie at the 7-yard line.

Tarkenton didn't waste any more opportunities. He hooked up with Foreman on a screen pass and the running back broke two tackles and made it all the way to the Rams' 12 before he was knocked out of bounds. Backup running back Sammy Johnson scored the final touchdown for the Vikings with 33 seconds to play.

1987: A PLAYOFF RUN TO REMEMBER

Not much was expected from the Vikings when they entered the 1987 playoffs as a wild-card team with an 8–7 record. They had finished three games behind the Chicago Bears in the NFC Central and Jerry Burns's team came stumbling to the regular-season finish line by losing three of their last four regular-season games.

While there were some major deficiencies on the defensive side, the Vikings had an offense that could move the ball in an explosive manner. Wade Wilson was the triggerman and he enjoyed an underrated crew of receivers that included Anthony Carter, Steve Jordan, Leo Lewis, and versatile running back Darrin Nelson.

One thing that the Vikings had going for them was that nobody expected anything from them. When they traveled to New Orleans to face Jim Mora, Bobby Hebert, and the 12–3 Saints, they were expected to run into a buzz saw. Not only had the Saints played consistently all season long, this was their first playoff game in team history.

But the Vikings were not in a cooperative mood. They came into the Superdome and laid a 44–10 beating on the Saints. The Vikings knew they were capable of an explosive offensive game—they had beaten the Cowboys 44–38 on Thanksgiving Day—but they had not demonstrated the consistency to put a big-time opponent away on the road.

New Orleans got on the board first when Hebert hit wideout Eric Martin with a 10-yard touchdown pass, but the Vikings defense went into shutdown mode from that point forward. They had four interceptions, two fumble recoveries, two sacks, and allowed only 149 total yards.

At the same time, Carter lit the fuse for the Vikings when he returned a punt 84 yards for a touchdown. He also caught a 10-yard touchdown pass from running back Allen Rice and Wade Wilson threw scoring passes to Jordan and the immortal Hassan Jones.

The game stunned the Saints. They had become the feel-good story of the year with their first winning season since their inception in 1967. However, after their destruction at the hands of the Vikings, they were once again the butt of jokes.

The next week, the Vikings went to Candlestick Park for a date with Joe Montana, Jerry Rice, and the powerful 49ers. Bill Walsh's team was the number one seed in the NFC with a 13–2 record and they looked across their rainy home field at the Vikings and sneered.

How could the Vikings stay on the field with the likes of Montana, Rice, Roger Craig, Tom Rathman, and John Frank? The 49ers could name their margin by halftime and just finish the game.

Somebody forgot to tell the Vikings. After the teams exchanged field goals in the first quarter, the Vikings reeled off 17 second-quarter points as Wilson hit tight end Carl Hilton with a seven-yard touchdown pass and rookie cornerback Reggie Rutland stole a Montana pass and returned it 45 yards for a score. The stunned 49ers could not come back and were tagged with a shocking 36–24 defeat.

The true hero for the Vikings was Carter once again. While he did not get into the end zone, he caught 10 passes for 227 yards on the sloppy field. "On a wet field like that, the receiver really has the advantage," Carter said. "The defensive backs really looked like they didn't want to slip and fall down. They were a little tentative."

The shocking loss stayed with the 49ers for a full season. They came back the next year using that game as motivation. They beat the Vikings and Bears in the playoffs before winning Super Bowl XXIII over the Bengals.

"Any time we ever felt tired the next season or felt like we needed a break we just thought of that game," said former 49ers guard Jesse Sapolu. "That game really hurt and it stayed with us."

That win sent the Vikings into the NFC championship game against a Redskins team that was starting to click with Doug Williams behind center, Timmy Smith running the ball, and Darrell Green in the secondary. The Redskins took a 17–10 lead late in the fourth quarter when Williams hit wideout Gary Clark with a seven-yard touchdown pass with 5:06 to go.

Wilson led the Vikings down the field, but a fourth-down pass to Nelson in the end zone was incomplete and the dream of returning to the Super Bowl died on the frozen dirt at RFK Stadium.

The Redskins used that game as a springboard to a 42–10 Super Bowl rout over the Broncos. After Denver took a 10–0 lead in the first quarter, the Redskins scored a record 35 points in the second quarter to put the game away.

It was the win over the Vikings that had hardened the Redskins. "Everyone knows how close we came to losing against the Vikings," said offensive lineman Russ Grimm. "That game hardened us and we were not going to let down after getting through against those guys."

Grant understood that the Rams were frustrated after outgaining the Vikings throughout the game. "They had a lot of adversity," Grant said of the Rams. "But my team has a way of creating adversity. We seem to find a way. It's a team game and this team played with more emotion than any of my other Viking teams."

Knox was angry and frustrated after the game, but he found the class to credit the Vikings for winning the NFC championship. "A great team finds a way to beat you," Knox said. "And one thing you have to say about the Vikings is that they do know how to win."

Grant's team was unable to sustain their winning ways against the Raiders in Super Bowl XI, but the 1976 Vikings were one of the most opportunistic teams the league has ever known. And that was because they made their own breaks from the beginning of the season to the end.

The Vikings beat the Los Angeles Rams in five of six playoff meetings, including one in Los Angeles. If only the Rams had been in the AFC and their postseason meetings had come in the Super Bowl. Impossible.

But the Vikings were glad to have one postseason patsy.

COMING OF AGE: OPPONENTS KNEW THEY WERE FOR REAL IF THEY COULD HANDLE THE VIKINGS

The Vikings rose from expansion team to solid organization relatively quickly in the NFL.

After starting their existence with three consecutive losing seasons, the Vikings were 8–5–1 in 1964 and the rest of the league took notice. Especially impressive that season were road wins over Vince Lombardi's Green Bay Packers and George Halas's Chicago Bears.

The Bears were the defending NFL champions but had fallen in '64. When they met the Vikings in the season finale at Wrigley Field, the Bears were ready to head into the off-season. Minnesota dominated Chicago 41–14 in a game that had Halas spewing bile afterward.

The win at Green Bay was even more remarkable. For their first three years, the Vikings were an entertaining expansion team led by scrambler Fran Tarkenton. But beating the Packers 24–23 in Green Bay in the fourth game of the season had a magical result. The Vikings walked back into the locker room with something they did not have at the start of the game: the confidence that comes with rising above their limitations. Shutting down Bart Starr, Jim Taylor, and the powerful Packers offensive line did wonders for the defense. The feeling permeated the locker room and the Vikings had grown up quite a bit.

The move from respectability to playoff team came four years later in 1968. The record might not have been impressive, but their 8–6 mark was good enough for them to win the NFC's Central Division. They lost to the Colts 24–14 in the postseason, but they would be in the Super Bowl the following year and remain one of the league's elite teams for more than 30 years. They might never have been able to win the Super Bowl—or even get back since the 1976 season—but they have always been a measuring stick for the rest of the league.

A win against Minnesota was usually hard earned and several championship teams gained their self-respect and self-confidence from wins over the Vikings.

In 1985 and 1986, the Bears and Giants won Super Bowl titles. Chicago's defensive ferocity combined with an opportunistic offense to form one of the best teams the league has ever seen. The Giants had a strong defense as well, but they weren't quite in Chicago's class. However, Bill Parcells had a significantly better offense in 1986 than the Bears had the year before.

Both were great teams by all standards and both got their confidence to win it all from wins over the Vikings.

In 1985 Chicago came into a nationally televised Thursday night game in the Metrodome to play Bud Grant's team. While it was an early season game, both undefeated (2–0) teams couldn't wait to get at each other. Bears middle linebacker Mike Singletary had gotten into fights during practice the week of the game and prepared for the Vikings by saying it was the "biggest game of our lives."

There was no love from the Minnesota side, particularly from Grant toward Bears coach Mike Ditka. Grant did not think Ditka had truly deserved the Bears head-coaching slot when he got it prior to the 1982 season and that he had parlayed his personal relationship with Halas into getting the job offer. "It's not what you know, it's who you know," Grant said.

Ditka was not one to let bygones be bygones. He remembered every slight, insult, and critical comment as if they had been war wounds. He believed that his team had the ability to dominate Minnesota on the field, but that wasn't enough for Ditka. He wanted to take a swipe at Grant's pregame insistence on his team's soldier-straight decorum during the national anthem.

Grant had grown tired of seeing Vikings opponents meander and fidget while the "Star-Spangled Banner" was played and he insisted his team stand at attention as the anthem was played. Prominent announcers like Curt Gowdy and Pat Summerall had praised the Vikings for their "class" and Ditka took notice. He told his team to stand at attention with their helmets in their left hand and their right hands over their hearts. "We'll see which team has more class," Ditka told his team.

The game itself had quite a bit of controversy from the Bears' perspective because their number one quarterback, Jim McMahon, had not been able to practice in the days leading up to the game because of a bad back and an infection. When Ditka let McMahon know that backup Steve Fuller would be starting, McMahon threw a fit. When the game began, he was sulking on the sidelines.

The Bears took a 6–3 lead, but the Vikings were not about to be intimidated. Tommy Kramer would have one of the best games of his career, throwing for 436 yards. He threw two touchdown passes and the Vikings had a 17–9 lead in the third quarter.

The normally overpowering Bears defense was getting beaten soundly. All-Pro defensive end Dan Hampton took the defensive backs to task on the sidelines, telling them to start "covering somebody."

Bears cornerback Leslie Frazier was not one to take criticism from a teammate in the middle of the game and shot back at Hampton, "Why don't you do your job and get after Kramer?"

On the offensive side, Fuller had completed 13 of 18 passes, but there was no spark. McMahon confronted Ditka on the sidelines and insisted that his coach put him in the game. The two exchanged heated words, but eventually McMahon got his wish.

Ditka was fearful that McMahon was not ready to play and would get hurt more seriously. He called for a screen pass and told McMahon he wanted him to play conservatively. But as McMahon went into his backpedal, he stumbled and nearly went to the ground. That threw off the timing of the screen. At the same time, Vikings linebacker Scott Studwell was blitzing McMahon and none of the Chicago offensive linemen were

TRIVIA

Who holds the record for the longest punt in Vikings history?

Find the answers on pages 193–194.

prepared to block him. An instant before he could smash into McMahon and possibly wreck his season, running back Walter Payton stepped up and hit the onrushing Studwell with a perfect block and stopped him cold. Rarely had a running back's block on a blitzing linebacker been so perfectly executed.

McMahon knew that the blitz had left speedy Willie Gault with one-on-one coverage and he launched a deep pass down the left side of the field. Gault caught it in stride and took it into the end zone for a 70-yard touchdown.

That play took away Minnesota's momentum and transferred it to the Bears. After a Vikings turnover, McMahon hit wide receiver Dennis McKinnon with a short touchdown pass to give the Bears the lead. Chicago would go on to win the game 33–24.

That was the game that gave the nation a Bears team that would destroy the New England Patriots 46–10 in Super Bowl XX. The Bears knew that they had a quarterback with moxie, guts, and the ability to make things happen when the game was on the line. After the Minnesota game, the rest of the league knew it as well.

A year later, the Giants were on an 8–2 roll when they came into the Metrodome to face a Vikings team that would finish the season 9–7. Minnesota had a very solid passing game with Tommy Kramer throwing to explosive Anthony Carter, dependable Leo Lewis, and solid tight end Steve Jordan. They had beaten the Bears at home and were confident when the Giants came to town.

With 1:12 to go in the fourth quarter, the Vikings were leading 20–19 and had the Giants gasping for air. New York had the ball at its own 47 and it was fourth-and-17. The Vikings dropped eight men into the secondary and New York quarterback Phil Simms was scouring the field for an open receiver. He could not find one, but as his protection was starting to break down, he threw a 22-yard completion to wide receiver Bobby Johnson to keep the game alive. The Giants took advantage of their fourth-down conversion when place-kicker Raul Allegre came in and kicked his fifth field goal of the game for a 22–20 New York victory.

TRIVIA

Who holds the Vikings record for most field goals in a game?

Find the answers on pages 193–194.

That game lit a fire within Simms. Until that point he had been a disappointment to Giants fans that had been waiting for their "phenom" to play winning football. The week before he had been eight of 18 in a 17–14 win over the Eagles and had been criticized thoroughly.

New York coach Bill Parcells knew his team would have no chance to beat the Vikings on the road if his quarterback was down on himself. He called Simms into his office to build his quarterback's self-esteem.

"I don't want you to pay any attention to anything that is written or said," Parcells said. "Because you are a great quarterback."

TRIVIA

Which two Vikings share the record for most points in a game?

Find the answers on pages 193–194.

Parcells told his quarterback to take chances on the field and dare the opposing defense to stop him. "Don't be cautious," Parcells said.

After leading the game-winning drive against Minnesota with his laser-like pass to Johnson, Giant fans believed in him. Parcells thought Simms' pass to Johnson was the key moment for his team.

"It really kick-started us to the Super Bowl," Parcells recalled. "It showed what we could do on the road against a good team under adverse circumstances. If we could do it then, we knew we could do it again."

Wins over the Vikings had given the Bears and Giants the inner belief that they could be world champions. The team and long-suffering Vikings fans are still waiting for their own championship-defining moment.

PAIN AND SUFFERING

SUPER BOWL: THE WRONG APPROACH

Bud Grant might have been the classy leader of the Vikings for 18 seasons, but his teams came undone in the four Super Bowls the Vikings played in.

The Vikings were heavily favored to uphold the honor of the NFL in Super Bowl IV against Kansas City, but they were in against very talented and very physical teams when they met the Dolphins, Steelers, and Raiders in their subsequent appearances. Grant is the last man to make any excuses, but the Vikings might have been in over their heads in all of those games.

Start with Super Bowl IV against the Chiefs. The Vikings had incredible pressure on them to regain the honor of the NFL after the Baltimore Colts lost to the American Football League's New York Jets the year before. While many NFL supporters were claiming that the game was a fluke and were boldly stating that the Vikings would mop up Tulane Stadium with the Chiefs, several league insiders were afraid of another embarrassment.

The Jets victory had emboldened the other AFL teams and this was their last game before they would join the NFL. One other factor favored the Chiefs—they were a bigger, stronger team that was able to lean on and push around its smaller rivals.

That's exactly how it played out as the Chiefs rolled 23–7. The Chiefs' front seven pummeled Joe Kapp, much the same way the

Dolphins and Steelers punished Fran Tarkenton in subsequent Super Bowls.

The 1973 Dolphins and 1974 Steelers are widely considered two of the greatest NFL dynasties of all time. Steve Sabol of NFL Films listed the four greatest football dynasties as the 49ers of the 1980s, the Dolphins and Steelers of the 1970s, and the Packers of the 1960s.

The Raiders were perhaps the hungriest team in professional sports when they met the Vikings in Super Bowl XI in the Rose Bowl. Al Davis had built a championship-caliber team 10 years earlier, but they had not gotten back to the Super Bowl since their appearance against Green Bay in Super Bowl II. John Madden had a superb team that had just beaten the dominant Steelers to get an opportunity to gain their first championship. They were primed and took advantage of every mistake by the Vikings.

TRIVIA

Who holds the Vikings record for most 50-or-more-yard field goals in a career?

Find the answers on pages 193–194.

So the Vikings might not have been as good as any of the teams they faced in their Super Bowl appearances. But there is one other factor to consider. The demeanor of Grant on pro football's brightest stage was not conducive to creating a winning atmosphere for his team.

Retired NFL executive director Don Weiss, who was charged with the responsibility of running the Super Bowls, recalls Grant as an uptight leader who was never happy about the responsibilities that go with an appearance in the championship game.

"We bent over backward trying to do things for Bud that people who worked for him told us he wanted, only to have Bud later complain that he hadn't wanted that at all," Weiss wrote in *The Making of the Super Bowl*. "He was uptight about all kinds of little things. I guess it was just his nature. He was a big believer in team concepts as a coach, as his teams demonstrated. As a person, however, he didn't take direction too well."

The Vikings players and assistant coaches clearly took their lead from their head coach. While he was in control during the regular season and in the playoffs, he was clearly just a soldier following orders when his team played in the Super Bowl. He didn't like it and he made no effort to hide his impatience with NFL officials.

"If we told Bud that he was to be someplace between 10 and 11 in the morning and that his AFC counterpart would follow him from 11 to noon, he would invariably ask why he had to go first and couldn't he go second," Weiss said. "If we explained our rationale for scheduling press conferences in the morning and team workouts in the afternoon to help the writers meet their daily deadlines, Bud would always ask why. He wanted things changed to suit his schedule and we couldn't do that just for him."

Who holds the Vikings record for sacks in a career?
Find the answers on pages 193–194.

Grant was particularly upset before the Vikings faced the Dolphins in Super Bowl VIII at Houston's Rice Stadium. During the week preceding the game, the Dolphins got to practice at the Oilers' headquarters and workout facility. The Vikings, on the other hand, used a high school facility several miles away. The decision on where each team practiced was determined by the luck of the draw, but Grant was not happy.

Even though the high school was very modern and Grant had both a grass field and artificial turf at his disposal, he was not pleased. "When Bud first arrived there, a sparrow had made its way into the locker room," Weiss said. "Grant immediately told the press that the NFL had put him in a bird sanctuary."

NFL officials who had put in many hours securing a first-rate facility for the team were enraged that Grant would bust their chops in such an embarrassing manner.

It wasn't any better for Grant, who would see his team fall behind 14–0 in the first quarter and suffer a 24–7 defeat at the hands of Don Shula and the Dolphins. The Dolphins defense looked good even compared with Minnesota's staunch defense, which had allowed just 168 points during the year. The Vikings

CHUCK FOREMAN: THE BEST PLAYER NOT IN THE HALL OF FAME

The ultimate do-it-all player to ever play the game might have been Walter Payton.

"Sweetness" was a runner with speed and power, could catch passes like a wideout, block like a demon, and throw passes when called upon.

He was the best player on an ordinary team for the majority of his career, but he was able to enjoy one of the greatest seasons of all time when the Bears went 15–1 in 1985 and won Super Bowl XX with a 46–10 win over New England.

Next in that discussion among most pro football "experts" is Marshall Faulk, who was a hold-your-breath kind of player with both the Colts and the Rams. He was nearly unstoppable in 1999 and the Rams won the Super Bowl that season with a thrilling win over the Titans.

The forgotten man in that discussion is Chuck Foreman. He played on some outstanding Vikings teams during his eight-year career from 1973–80. The Vikings went to the playoffs seven times in his career but never came away with the big prize. Perhaps that explains why Foreman does not have a bronze bust in the Hall of Fame.

He was a great player who had a style that was part Gale Sayers, part Barry Sanders, and 100 percent excitement. The sight of No. 44 in the open field with the ball under his arm was sheer joy for the Vikings and their fans, but it was terror to those trying to stop him.

"I hated playing against Foreman," said former Chicago Bears linebacker Doug Buffone, who has been a talk show host in Chicago throughout his post-football career. "He could make you look sick. With Foreman, you had to get him early. He was impossible to bring down in the open field. He had moves that looked great on film, but it was a horror show when you had to play against him.

"When you get to the NFL, it means you have some ability and you have accomplished something. But when you go up against a guy like Foreman, he could make you feel like you didn't belong. Inept is the word. The only thing that made you feel better is that he did it to everybody."

Foreman played in an era when defenses were dominant. He was the NFC player of the year in 1974 and 1976. His 1975 season was one of

185

the best in NFL history. He ran for 1,070 yards and 13 touchdowns and caught 73 passes for 691 yards and nine more scores.

During his era, he was the player opposing coaches feared as game day approached. He was dominant in all phases of the offense and should be in the Hall of Fame. He ran for 5,950 yards and 3,156 receiving yards and scored 76 touchdowns.

Critics point out that his career that was cut short by injuries. His last two seasons, he was a shell of the player that he had been earlier. However, that didn't stop the Hall of Fame selectors from voting Sayers into the Hall of Fame. Sayers had a seven-year career, and only five of them were productive. While it's clear that Sayers's numbers would have been much better if

Chuck Foreman had an array of skills and moves that made him a joy to Vikings fans and a terror to opponents.

he had not suffered a devastating knee injury midway through the 1968 season, the fact remains that his numbers are not as good as Foreman's totals. Sayers ran for 4,956 yards and 39 touchdowns in his career.

Sayers was a brilliant athlete who scored six touchdowns in a legendary game in the mud against the 49ers as a rookie in 1965. Foreman never had that kind of game, but during the 1975 season he had five games with three or more touchdowns.

The comparison is apt and there is no doubt that Sayers was a spectacular player who belongs in the shrine. But so does the great Chuck Foreman. His absence from Canton is something that today's Hall of Fame selectors need to address.

It's not just the numbers. Take a look at the films. He belongs there as much as any of the great running backs.

It's time to get him bronzed.

were never able to come up with any kind of answer in what might have been the dullest Super Bowl of them all.

Grant's attitude during the four Super Bowls might not have been the determining factor in his team's Super Bowl losses, but it certainly didn't help the Vikings come up with any peak efforts against any of their opponents.

It's the only black mark on his otherwise sterling résumé. Unfortunately for him, it's the one thing that fans most associate with him.

TRAGEDY AT TRAINING CAMP: THE LOSS OF KOREY STRINGER

During the Vikings' memorable 15–1 season in 1998, the unsung stars were the offensive linemen who consistently gave Randall Cunningham time to survey the field and find open receivers. The unit included left tackle Todd Steussie, left guard Corbin Lacina, center Matt Birk, right guard David Dixon, and right tackle Korey Stringer.

Dixon and Stringer were particularly large and powerful men. Whenever the Vikings needed to make a yard on third or fourth down or were in tight around the goal line, the Vikings loved to send running backs Robert Smith and Leroy Hoard to the right side and particularly over Stringer.

Selected by the Vikings in the first round of the 1995 draft, Stringer quickly showed the league that a right tackle could be worth a first-round pick, starting 15 games in his rookie year. At 6'4" and 340 pounds, Stringer was a mountain of a man with the strength and ability to match his size. He had problems with his weight during his college career at Ohio State, but got that problem under control as his career progressed.

Stringer had a superior season in 2000, winning a spot on the NFC Pro Bowl team. Head coach Dennis Green and offensive line coach Mike Tice expected more of the same from Stringer in 2001. Stringer had proved to be quite durable, averaging 15 starts per season in his first six years.

Stringer was not much different than a lot of NFL veterans who hated the rigors of training camp. The summer of 2001 proved to be hot and humid and the conditions were particularly nasty at the Vikings' training camp in Mankato, Minnesota.

TRIVIA

Who holds the Vikings record for longest return with an interception?

Find the answers on pages 193–194.

On the first day of training camp, Stringer struggled with the heat and conditions and had to be carted off the field. The next day, August 1, Stringer was determined to prove it was just a matter of adjusting to the conditions.

However, there was no adjustment as the big man vomited three times but didn't call for the team's training staff until the practice was over. He was brought to an air-conditioned trailer that served as the team's training room, where he quickly lost consciousness.

Paramedics took Stringer to Immanuel St. Joseph's–Mayo Health Center with a frightening body temperature of 108.8 degrees. The most immediate need was to bring Stringer's body temperature down. He was dipped into tubs of icy water. Towels were dipped in the water and then draped over his body and wadded up and tucked under his armpits.

Korey Stringer leaves the field after a game during the 2000 season. Stringer died of heat stroke on August 1, 2001, a day after he collapsed at the team's training camp. The 335-pound Pro Bowl tackle developed symptoms of heat stroke, including weakness and rapid breathing, following the team's morning practice, when the heat index reached 110 degrees.

As the day moved on, as many as 15 physicians—including cardiologists, a pulmonologist, a critical-care physician, and a kidney specialist—were working on Stringer.

The Pro Bowl offensive tackle appeared to make progress, but during the evening he developed a heatstroke-related bleeding condition that prevents the blood from clotting. Stringer began to bleed internally. He responded well to treatment for the condition, but then his kidneys began to fail.

He was put on dialysis twice and his doctors thought he was making progress. But then his organs began to give out. He needed help breathing and was put on a respirator. And then at 10:00 PM, his heart began to fail.

"We thought we had turned a corner, but then his heart gave out and there was nothing we could do," said Dr. David Knowles, who coordinated Stringer's treatment.

"The people at the hospital, they did the most unbelievable job to try to recapture his life," said grieving wide receiver Cris Carter, who stayed at the hospital throughout Stringer's ordeal. "There are just certain forces in nature you just can't change."

Despite the best efforts of a team of physicians and specialists, Stringer never regained consciousness and died early the next morning. The heartbreaking loss sent the Vikings into shock and they never recovered during the season. The team was grief-stricken and in the immediate hours after Stringer's death, Carter, Green, and Randy Moss met with the media and all three broke down.

Minnesota Vikings head coach Dennis Green (right) wipes away tears on Wednesday, August 1, 2001, as he and players Cris Carter (left) and Randy Moss (center) address a news conference concerning Korey Stringer. Pro Bowl tackle Stringer died of heat stroke a day after collapsing at the Vikings' training camp on the hottest day of the year.

The only other NFL training camp fatality was J.V. Cain, a tight end for the St. Louis Cardinals, who died of a heart attack on July 22, 1979. Chuck Hughes, a wide receiver for the Detroit Lions, died of a heart attack October 24, 1971, during a game in Detroit against the Chicago Bears.

TRIVIA

Who is the Vikings career leader in tackles?

Find the answers on pages 193–194.

Stringer's friendly, fun-loving personality made the loss even tougher to accept. He used to crack his teammates up with his Jim Carrey–esque impressions of Tice and Green. He did the impressions with a little bit of edge, but it was clear that Stringer was just trying to have fun and make his teammates laugh. Both coaches bore the imitations with good humor.

Tice was particularly affected by Stringer's death. In addition to being protective and proud of all the Vikings offensive linemen, he was particularly close to Stringer. Tice cried when he heard that Stringer had died and called his death "the toughest thing" in his life.

"I lost my favorite 'baby' and my son," Tice said.

Stringer also regularly gave back to the community. He would visit classrooms in the Minneapolis–St. Paul metropolitan area and simply volunteer to help. He regularly espoused the theory that "when you read, you lead," and that endeared him to teachers and students alike. Stringer volunteered at the Bancroft Elementary School in Minneapolis for five years.

Teacher Carol Dey said some athletes and celebrities would visit the school once or maybe twice, but Stringer showed up regularly for a significant period of time.

Stringer promoted literacy and local involvement as part of his "Korey's Crew," a community program he started.

Dey said Stringer wasn't like other celebrities who have volunteered in her classroom. The huge lineman would sit among the fifth graders and ask what they were reading.

One year, the class had a display of a Viking's head with a braid that each student could attach a piece of paper to every time they read a book. Stringer challenged the kids to extend the braid to the principal's office down the hall, which they eagerly did.

Toward the end of the 2000–01 school year, Stringer came back and celebrated the feat with pizza, Dey said.

"He was a friend. He was a genuine friend from another world," she said. "It was a great loss to our school and our community."

Even opponents—those who regularly went to battle against Stringer and knew the damage his strong hands could do while blocking—missed him significantly. Former Packers defensive tackle Santana Dotson said he had an empty feeling when he walked out onto the Metrodome turf in October 2001. "We had some major battles on the field and it just felt so empty without him on the field," said Dotson. "We didn't talk a lot—other than four-letter insults—but I respected him so much."

As powerful and dominating as he could be on the field, he was as gentle off of it. He left behind a wife and child who cherished him greatly. On the field he was a powerful giant who could muscle and maul his opponents. The loss on the field was huge, but it didn't compare to what the Stringer or Vikings families felt in their hearts.

TRIVIA ANSWERS

Page 6: 1984, 3–13

Page 11: Steve Jordan, 178, and Stu Voigt, 131

Page 14: Gary Anderson, 35

Page 17: Tommy Mason, 1961

Page 22: Chuck Foreman in 1975

Page 25: January 28, 1960; they were allowed to begin play in 1961. The day before, the Vikings organization renounced their application to become a charter member of the American Football League.

Page 31: Bud Grant was elected to the Hall in 1994

Page 34: 1967–83, 1985; 168–108–5 (including 10–12 in the postseason)

Page 42: Harry

Page 45: November 5, 1995, against the Green Bay Packers

Page 58: Fran Tarkenton in 1986

Page 61: 1961–66; 29–51–4

Page 64: Cris Carter, 122 (1994)

Page 71: Cris Carter; 111

Page 74: Once, in 1961

Page 79: 1986–91; 55–46–0 (including 3–3 in the postseason)

Page 81: Alan Page had two safeties in 1971

Page 83: Running back Tommy Mason

Page 86: December 5, 1993, when they beat Detroit 13–0

Page 90: Bud Grant, Jerry Burns, and Dennis Green

Page 94: 1964, a 24–23 win

Page 97: Norm Van Brocklin, "the Dutchman"

Page 100: Week 2 of the 1976 season; the game was a 10–10 tie against the Los Angeles Rams at the Met

Page 102: "The Stiffs"

Page 112: Fran Tarkenton (1975) and Randall Cunningham (1998)

Page 118: 1992–2001; 101–70–0 (4–8 in the postseason)